Restarts, Mulligans, and Do-Overs

# GIVING FAITH A SECOND CHANCE

## CHRISTOPHER B. WOLF

FaithWalk
PUBLISHING
Grand Haven, Michigan

Published in association with the literary agency of Credo Communications, LLC, Grand Rapids, Michigan, 49525.

Printed in the United States of America

12 11 10 09 08 07          7 6 5 4 3 2 1

Library of Congress Cataloging-in-Publication Data

Wolf, Christopher B.
    Giving faith a second chance : restarts, Mulligans, and do-overs / Christopher B. Wolf.
        p. cm.
    ISBN-13: 978-1-932902-68-6 (pbk. : alk. paper)
    ISBN-10: 1-932902-68-6
    1. Church work with ex-church members. 2. Ex-church members. I. Title.
    BV4013.W65 2007
    248.8′4–dc22

                           2007014124

To my Mark 5 sisters who are
still suffering, hiding, or sleeping;
to my brothers who have yet to come home.


"And he arose and came to his father. But while he was
yet at a distance, his father saw him and had compassion,
and ran and embraced him and kissed him."

—Luke 15:20 RSV

For Doug + Barb:
Thank God for the
the two of you! You
have been such a blessing
to us —
        love,
        Christoph

# Contents

# THE INVITATION

How is it that we can feel like it all seems so impossible and at the same time makes so much sense ?

That is how I feel about sharing this message with you. There was little in my past to suggest that I would become a pastor. Growing up, my family and friends predicted that I would become a priest, but always in a mocking manner because of my lack of girlfriends and my serious side.

The irony is that my "ministry" of walking with people through suffering, pain, and despair began with the very people who were kidding me about being a priest. In some ways, I have been a "minister" since I was ten years old. Already I was listening to and encouraging struggling family members.

At the same time I was learning about Jesus and wondering how he fit into the unique things I was experiencing. From the beginning I have had an on-again/off-again relationship with church. Growing up Roman Catholic, I loved Mass and the Sacraments, but as I matured I felt I needed more than a top-down approach to faith—one more anchored in the Bible.

Today I love my job as a pastor, but it is crushing to know that so many people stay home on Sunday morning because of the way churches, pastors, and priests have treated them. Even as one of "them," I am trying to do things differently, though it doesn't change the reality for so many. Jesus's message to "come as you are" doesn't always jibe with what churches and pastors communicate: "You don't fit here." I love the power and authenticity of true worship, but it's grating when worship becomes showy and unreal. And I love all that a church can be—a kind of heaven on earth— but am dismayed at how rarely it achieves this. At one point I walked away from the church because it was about everything else but the heart.

And so here I am, a pastor now. But it's not about the seminary training, title, or duties. It is all about the heart. A heart broken by life and all that comes with it—the grief, the confusion, the disillusionment. A heart that is still breaking when people feel like God has forgotten them, or when they conclude that second chances are impossible. And without the hope of a do-over, people like you and me find ourselves at the end of our ropes.

*Desperate. Empty. Trapped. Forsaken.* These are words that describe that end-of-the-rope experience. There is the unsettling sensation of suspending between faith and doubt, worth and worthlessness, sacred and stained, whole and broken, secure and scared. Even worse—at the end of our rope we just don't know which way to reach. But as we will see together, there is a reason for it all.

Out of my own broken pieces, I now ache and reach out to others who are suffering and trapped and feeling forsaken. The desire to write this book could only come from a heart that has lost a lot of precious things, suffered at times, and carried the grief of many other hearts—and is still filled with hope . . . abundant hope!

I think of a woman who had never trusted anyone else before. She lived in impossible circumstances. But I had the opportunity and desire to reach out to her, to extend my hand into her prison cell. The experience was difficult and bewildering at times, but also hopeful and wondrous, though I was never quite sure how my efforts made a difference. But that wasn't the point. The point was the reach, the desire to meet her despair with my compassion, which flowed from my own pain and brokenness. This is how God works—offering healing and grace and second chances to journey through broken circumstances.

Earlier this year, I got an email from this same woman, and in it she wrote:

> "I was once crushed . . . at the end of my rope,
> but this person I know, he showed me the way back,
> the way back to our Lord's nearness and hope."

The end of one's rope is an awful and lonely place—no matter why you are there. This is the time to uncover some things about God you may have never known or believed. And along the way you may see the possibilities of giving faith a second chance. Not faith in church or other people, but faith in God.

Your whole life has been building up to this moment when everything can make sense even when it seems impossible.

So no matter how long it has been for you, no matter how empty you feel, no matter how far away you've gone—please take my hand.

## Part One

## We Are ... Desperate

"It's just that I'm at the end of my rope. I can't do this anymore, CB," Karen tearfully whispered. I pressed the receiver closer to my ear as I struggled for an answer, but I knew there just wasn't one—this time. I prayed that the Lord would supply me with wise and comforting words. But nothing came. All I could do was listen as she began to weep—again. This was not our first conversation like this. But this one was different—she really was at the end of her rope.

At the end of our rope we feel forsaken. It is a fearful existence. No matter how far away we have run from the Lord, the thought and sensation of then being abandoned and forgotten by God is terrifying and paralyzing. But we also feel deserted, alienated by others. We feel left behind not only by family and friends, but also church families and congregations in whom many of us trusted. Many of the same people who promised to love and care for us judge us for the things we have done; they make us feel inadequate, unacceptable, and unwelcome. The rope end is so isolated; it feels like there is no one around, no one even close enough to cry out to.

We feel trapped—trapped by circumstances as well as our own decisions and choices. We also feel trapped by all the anger. Things have gone wrong and haven't made sense. After a while, it all starts to pile up. The wreckage, the sins, the guilt, the rage, and the tragedies—they all pull us further and further down. The weight of it all is life draining.

"I've got nothing left," people have told me many times. And it is such a strange feeling—this emptiness. We feel emptied of life, of purpose, of energy and hope. Even worse, we can scarcely detect our souls. The simple routines of life and religion can make us feel so spiritually barren, like we have a huge hole inside. No matter how hard we try to fill it—it just keeps sucking in hope but never fills us back up.

All of this, the alienation, the weight, and the desolation create a perfect storm of desperation inside. We are afraid and anxious; what should we do? When we are desperate, almost everything around us appears distorted—God, ourselves, people, and circumstances; it is so confusing. So meaningless. Where does it begin and end? At the end of our ropes, we can't decide whether to let go, or to try and climb up; and holding on is exhausting. We know we are at the end of the rope when we realize that there is nothing else we can do but hold on. We know we are at the end of the rope when we have been stripped of everything that used to work before.

Could there be something else going on here? I know we throw around the phrase, "There is a purpose to everything" a lot when we try to rationalize terrible things and times. But could there even be a purpose to being at the end of our rope? There might be. But for now, I know we're tired, I know it is so hard to trust, I know that we just want it to stop—but I am asking us to hold on just a little longer. Let's tie a knot at the end our ropes and rest awhile ...

# Chapter 1

## We Are
# Alienated

### You're in my seat!

"The deepest need of man is the need to overcome his separateness, to leave the prison of his aloneness."

—Erich Fromm

There is nothing like a Sunday morning in America.

All over the nation, on Sunday morning, people are getting ready. There is anticipation in the air. We put on our special Sunday morning attire. We want to get there early because it is a beautiful day. Everyone is going to want to be there ...

So, we get our bicycles and boats out; we head out to Home Depot for the supplies for that day's project; we run down to the store to get a newspaper; we take the dog for a long walk; we throw the stuff in the car for the tailgate party and drive like crazy to get our spot in the stadium parking lot; and we sleep off Saturday night's fun. Sunday morning in America is, as we could imagine, about freedom.

A retired colleague once said he was driving to attend worship and saw the mall parking lots filled on Sunday morning. What could make people exchange worshipping God for standing in checkout lines? Sunday mornings were once about the Lord; now they are more about getting done what we didn't during the week and taking time for ourselves.

At the same time, there are people at the end of their ropes that start thinking about going back to their church or trying a new one as a way of reconnecting with God. We dream of finding a way back to God—"This could be the day!" we think. And with a prayer and a deep breath, we stretch to grab the rope a little higher, hoping to rise a few feet from the end.

What many of them don't realize—and what we have learned quite well—is that there is a major obstacle standing in the way. It is well camouflaged. We never see it coming. It's name? The church member—the ultimate church protection system.

Church members have all sorts of techniques for making visitors and other members feel unwelcome. It's not all malicious. They believe they have good intentions. If we asked them, they would tell us that they are caring for and protecting "their" church (I thought it was Jesus's). Some of the defenses in their arsenals are quite effective. There is the ignoring method. Then there is the "slight seating adjustment" method where the church member ever so subtly moves away from the visitor. Makes us feel right at home when we get the impression that we are gross and unholy, right? There is also the "I am going to keep glaring at you until you take your crying baby and get out of here" method. And then there is the classic, "Let's all talk in our secret church code so that none of the visitors understand what we are talking about."

And the damage continues to be done by church folk when it comes to "welcoming" visitors. For many churches, visitors are welcome only if they stay to themselves and don't take members' seats and look "okay." It is a familiar story. It is an end of the rope tale.

At a church that needed to grow to survive, and was starting to grow, I once heard members say, "New members are taking over the church!"

There is an agonizing irony in the millions of stories and experiences of people reaching out from their rope end and hiding places hoping to meet God through a gathering of believers (theoretically representing hospitality and compassion). After all Jesus says, "... and anyone who comes to me I will never drive away;" (John 6:37). Shouldn't we expect churches of his name to reflect this same principle?

Of course what sends us stretching from the rope end— seeking—is the numbing pain of isolation. Naturally, most people there are going to try to find their way out from time to time by going to or going back to church. Community and the desire to belong are God-given. This is why the rope end is such an unnatural experience. We were intended to be in a relationship with God *and* other people.

Think about it. From the time we are young, we want to belong. We want to belong to our parents and then our friends and then perhaps to a spouse and a new family. It goes beyond family. Clubs, service organizations, and churches offer this sense of belonging. Why do so many corporations, retail, and grocery stores offer club or membership benefits—as if we "belong" to their club by being a customer? They are capitalizing on one of our most important human need—to belong, to fit in.

This is also why we also do extreme things, sometimes destructive things, just to belong. How many alcoholics of today were once young people who just wanted to fit in with the crowd?

Think back to Karen. When she called me in desperation, she was thirsting for belonging, hanging on for her life at the end of her rope. She was hoping to find a place to finally fit in. Like many, she drove by the church or saw the advertisement in the newspaper or phone book. And she thought, "Let me try again; I have to try again."

Karen braced herself, haunted by memories and unhealed scars, but undeterred because of this thirst for belonging. And it looked so perfect. The wondrous architecture, the glowing friendly faces, and the chirping organ prelude faintly echoing near the door were all drawing her closer.

The excited greeters at the door were so warm and welcoming. "We're glad you're here this morning," exclaimed the older gentleman who gave Karen's hand an extra squeeze as he handed her the bulletin.

"This could be it," she thought as a smile swept briefly across her face. She scanned the rows for an open seat. Not too close to people, but not hiding either.

Karen carefully and reverently negotiated her way into a pew and settled her posture into the stiff back of the seat. Her eyes were hypnotized by the people buzzing, the high ceiling, the big windows, and the magnificent cross. It was just as she remembered it … .

Karen began a prayer of thanksgiving to God. At the same time, though, the whispers started. She took someone's seat (in a place where there are no reserved seats). As hard as she tried, she couldn't escape the falling feeling that the very place that should be a sanctuary, her sanctuary, was just a mirage.

"That young woman is sitting in my seat!" growled an older woman to some others behind Karen, who turned from her prayer with shock to see who was speaking. Karen quickly turned back and froze. Her mind raced. "Should I move?" she thought. "Is this really her seat?"

What briefly appeared to be at least a refuge (if not a release) from her rope end, was an illusion. And she felt ashamed of the desire, the thirst that drove her there that morning as she felt her grip on the rope begin to slide.

So she stayed to be polite, but she wanted to run each time she sensed the waves of wrath from behind her. As Karen gazed upon the magnificent cross she thought and prayed, "*Why,* Jesus?" The whole service was a blur—a lost hour—and she ran out after the benediction.

Has anybody thought about how there are more open seats than ever in most traditional Christian churches today, yet so many of the seats are already "taken"? How can this be?

Why are we not going to church this Sunday? Why have we not gone back to church for years or decades? That's easy. Our seats are already taken.

On the other hand, the seating capacity here at the end of the rope is unlimited. But I hear there are huge lines over at Wal-Mart.

There is nothing like a Sunday morning in America.

## QUESTIONS

1.  What do you do on Sunday mornings?

    How is it different from when you were growing up?

2.  How do you experience your desire to belong?

    What do you do to fulfill this desire to belong?

3.  Have you ever felt unwelcome at a church or felt abandoned by Christians?

    Can you share what it feels like?

## CHAPTER 2

# WE ARE
# Estranged

## The resignation and exhaustion of being forgotten.

> "I give the fight up: let there be an end,
> A privacy, an obscure nook for me.
> I want to be forgotten even by God."
> —Robert Browning
> *Paracelsus, V*

You can almost always tell if someone really remembers you or not. Some are better actors than others. Some people can fake it, even if they can't remember your name. But, it's more in the face and the eyes. If someone really remembers you, there is a certain undeniable spark.

You see, if the essence of remembering is a kind of "keeping," then forgetting is a kind of letting go or neglecting. And I am not just talking about remembering names, facts, and figures.

There are those days when we look into the mirror and the reflection just doesn't look the same. We get to a point where we forget who we were and are. Holocaust survivor and Nobel Peace Prize winner Elie Weisel wrote about this in *Night*, the memoir of his experience in a concentration camp, "One day I was able to get up, after gathering all my strength. I wanted to see myself in the mirror hanging on the opposite wall. I had not seen myself since the ghetto.

From the depths of the mirror, a corpse gazed back at me. The look in his eyes, as they stared into mine, has never left me."[1] Life can be so devastating that we can scarcely identify the evidence left behind.

Our faces are revelations of our lives; they show if we have been remembered or forgotten. And when we feel forgotten by ourselves—a kind of self-initiated amnesia—there is a guise of resignation and exhaustion that replaces our true visage.

Forgetting happens with others, too. Think about the anticipation of attending your first high school reunion. The advantage I had going to my reunion was that I was a "late bloomer," so I looked a lot better at the reunion than I ever did at school. I detected surprise from a number of classmates. But more than admiration, when we go to reunions the hope is for recognition. The central question we want to know is "Did I matter as much to you as you did to me?"

That God, our creator, savior, and sustainer has forgotten us is a devastating thought. In order for us to believe this we also have to believe that we have done something or that something has happened to make us unrecognizable to him.

A verse from Scripture captures this feeling, "How long, O Lord? Will you forget me forever? How long will you hide your face from me?" (Psalm 13:1). God doesn't or wouldn't recognize me anymore? Could it be that our souls are not recognizable anymore—the sins, the guilt, the wounds, the doubts, the questions? Are these enough to disfigure our souls beyond recognition? It can't be true; except that it feels true. If I can barely recognize myself, if other people have long forgotten me, if my soul is on life support, and if I can't remember the last time I felt God's presence or anything remotely like God—maybe this is real.

The feeling of being forgotten and neglected and not kept by God is terribly real for so many. And if we're there it is not so far to then think that we must have no cosmic value. That is where a lot of people are today; purely at the end of the rope. It really feels like God is hiding his face from us.

## QUESTIONS

1. What are some words to describe the experience of feeling forgotten by God?

2. What do you see when you look in the mirror today?

   How has your image of yourself changed over the years?

3. Is there a connection between being forgotten and hiding?

   Can you say some more about that?

CHAPTER 3

WE ARE
# Ashamed

### Even after years,
### we all still peek out from our hiding places.

Remember playing hide and seek? I play it with my children Madelyn and Brian these days. As I creep softly through the hallway, the tension mounts. "Where are they this time? (The same places they always hide.) "Is he coming?" And then there is that quiet instant—maybe only a few seconds—that's a blend of suspense and wonder of being found or staying hidden. When I do find them there is lots of screaming and laughing—pure joy!

Many of us continue the hide and seek game as adults. Only as adults, it is not really a game. It becomes much more than that—it has a purpose to it. The end of our rope is also a great hiding place.

First comes the hiding and then comes the darkness.

Of course, we begin to hide for different reasons. We hide for protection—from a threat perhaps—and from shame. For some the hiding begins in youth. Just a little bit at first. I am not just talking about burying our faces in our mother's dresses or running to our bedrooms. We begin to learn to hide ourselves and our souls.

Author and speaker John Bradshaw defines shame-driven hiding in this way: "At the deepest level toxic shame triggers our basic automatic defensive cover-ups. Freud called these automatic cover-ups our primary ego defenses. Once these defenses are in place they function automatically and unconsciously, sending our true and authentic self into hiding."[1]

Whether it is because of protection or shame, as a child or an adult, the need to hide serves our bodies, souls, and minds. There was a time in my life when I did some serious hiding. I had severe acne from about age fifteen to nineteen. The deep red and purple cysts felt like tumors and were often sore; they were slow to heal and usually left scars. Comments like, "What happened to your face?" didn't help. I went to a dermatologist for most of those years—for more pain and humiliation. Sitting in the waiting room with my affliction literally writtten on my face wasn't even the worst part. Enduring injections into the cysts and having whiteheads pinched out of my skin followed. Antibiotics, Accutane, creams, and treatments did little to help.

There was a time, for about a year, that I couldn't look in a mirror. Literally. If I caught my reflection in a shop window I quickly looked away. How many times did I ask God why this was happening? To say I was dispirited and distant would be an understatement. I was in hiding. I was protecting myself from the thoughts and perceptions of others and from rejection and just feeling ashamed.

Many of you are in hiding as the result of things much worse than acne. What is hiding like for the rape or molestation victim? What is hiding like for a widow or widower? What is hiding like for the unemployed? What is hiding like for the teenage girl who has been rejected by her friends? What is hiding like for an alcoholic?

We also hide because we don't want people to find out about our sins and mistakes. Sometimes we get to the point where we think we have sinned so much that there are too many to be forgiven. We believe we have exceeded the sin limit for God to forgive.

It is a separation on our part; a kind of lockdown. Our schools today go into lockdown because of threatening situations in or near them. Turtles and snails retreat into their shells. Same thing.

It is the same thing that drove Jesus's disciples into hiding after his crucifixion (John 20:19). Although they had the news of Jesus being risen, their doubts and fears drove them behind locked doors in the dark of night.

First comes the hiding and then comes the darkness.

Like the disciples we get lost, stuck, and confused. One thing about the end of the rope is this: It is a refuge from the question of God being all that God is promised to be. In the disciples' case, they had believed to some degree that Jesus had been the Messiah. When it appeared otherwise, they sought protection in hiding and then darkness—turning inward.

Many of us grow up with an image of Jesus being a helpful friend who is "always there." And then along the way, we learn that faith takes much more to hold onto. Understandably, this realization can be so unbearable that we run and hide in the darkness rather than face it.

The darkness acts as a lid over our hiding places. In the darkness, there is no risk and therefore no faith. In the darkness, there is little certainty—vision is fuzzy at best. Darkness may dim our hopes and expectations, but the pain of the disappointment remains. In the darkness, our sins and mistakes are much less visible. With the illusion of security, darkness provides the perfect conditions for wounds and isolation to blossom. Very few things that are healthy grow in the dark.

Isn't faith that thing in life which is supposed to be about wholeness, hope, and security? Is it any wonder that so many of us would find ourselves hiding under cover of darkness at the end of our rope?

We even learn how to hide from God in his own house. Sometimes a congregation can have a "head in the sand" approach to members' problems. It might be that nobody talks about problems—so that they always remain hidden. So the place where hurts and challenges should be shared (Galatians 6:2), where the proclaimed "truth shall set us free" (John 8:32) can unintentionally become one of the best hiding places.

And yet, like the disciples' modern-day counterparts, with the doors locked, in the dark, we can still hear words of that familiar voice: "Peace be with you" (John 20:19).

Apparently, our hiding and darkness and locked doors can usually keep us human beings out, but can't keep Jesus out.

Here's the thing—the irony of hiding and darkness is that as deep and consuming as it can be, its power can be undone by just a spark, a shaft of light, a loving word or a reach. And so it is for the soul.

Isn't hide and seek about being found? As much effort as Madelyn and Brian put into hiding—don't they also want to be found? What kind of fun would it be if it was just called "hide?" The hiding is the catalyst but the seeking and finding is the resolution.

What drives us to hide and cover ourselves with darkness is real. The fears, the questions, the sins, the shame. But even after years, decades, we all still peek out from our hiding places, from the darkness, from the pew, to see if someone is coming. And we exist in this place of dread or longing because we have to—because it may be all we have.

## QUESTIONS

1. What are some of the things that have sent you into hiding?

2. What is it like to feel stuck between wanting to be found and wanting to stay hidden?

3. Can we be driven to hide so deeply that we feel like we are in the depths of our souls?

   What is that like?

CHAPTER 4

WE ARE
# Grieving

The cry may be universal prayer. No eloquence, no great words …

"The pain thus grows to such a degree that in spite of herself the sufferer gives vent to loud cries, which she cannot stifle, however patient and accustomed to pain she might be, because this is not a pain which is felt in the body, but in the depths of the soul."

—Teresa of Avila

"Maybe they aren't going to play it," I thought as the ushers escorted us down the aisle away from the altar. And then the familiar first notes started and I braced myself.

It was my mother Kathleen's funeral service, and we had selected "The Wind Beneath My Wings"[1] as the last song—the same song to which she and I danced at my wedding six years earlier.

*"It must have been cold there in my shadow …"* the deep voice echoed throughout the sanctuary.

I heard the words and the music and I began to experience a spiritual and physical sensation I had never felt before. It was a strong urge to collapse. I now wonder if it was some kind of breakdown. The meaning of the song, the memory of dancing with her and now her lying in a casket, the sense of defeat, the absurdity of her death, the anguish, and the angry questions for God all swirled around me. I wanted to just let go and die—right there in the middle of the church ... the same church where I had come to know God; the same church where I had walked down the aisle for my first communion and my confirmation; the same church where I broke into pieces at her father's funeral almost fifteen years earlier.

My legs kept moving, but everything was in slow motion. I stayed upright, but something had changed; something had left me in an impenetrable state of emptiness and pain, defeat and helplessness.

That is the thing about the rope's end. You can be wherever you are—at your job, with your family and friends, at a movie, wherever, and literally be at the end of your rope—and it can go almost unnoticed. And so what else can you do when you are suffering and feeling helpless and crushed? "Out of the depths I cry to you, O Lord. Lord hear my voice! Let your ears be attentive to the voice of my supplications" (Psalm 130: 1–2).

Sometimes all we can do is cry out from the depths. Is it enough? No. Will it make the pain go away? No. Will it make us feel better at all? Not clear. Sometimes all we can do is cry out from the depths.

And so we need to cry out from the funeral. We need to cry out when the beatings start again. We need to cry out when the bills can't be paid.

Newborns cry out. According to one child rearing book, "Crying is, after all, the only way infants have of communicating their needs and feelings—their very first baby talk. Your baby can't tell you that she's lonely, hungry, wet, tired, uncomfortable, too warm, too cold, or frustrated in any other way."[2]

We are no longer newborns or infants, but spiritually speaking, we all have these times in our lives when we can't find the words. There may literally be no words for what we are feeling or experiencing.

What is the vocabulary for grief? What is the terminology for expressing helplessness? What are the terms for total defeat—physical, mental and spiritual?

As C.S. Lewis once wrote, "I not only live each endless day in grief, but live each day thinking about living each day in grief."[3] This is to be at the depths—when there are no more words to capture the state of souls. When a cry is all that arises. It is spiritually primal.

You see, we were designed to be in relationship with God—attached to God. To be connected to God is the ultimate human existence. So when we are crying out from the depths and feel that we are the furthest distance from God and others, it is an incomparable pain. The incomparable pain comes and often stays because we are at the very opposite end of the spectrum of spiritual existence. The pain of feeling separated from God—even if we have never known him or have purposefully avoided him. We may be able to trick our minds, but we can't fool our souls about who and what we are. A relationship with God can be so fulfilling; it is designed to be that way; that is why the opposite—separation—is so hard.

There is this great children's book, *Am I Praying?* in which a little boy named Erik has a terrible day—forgets his lunch and gets separated from his class on a trip—and he keeps asking if his various thoughts count as prayers. At one point he asks Jesus, "Why aren't you helping me? Is that a prayer, too?"[4] The answer for Erik and for us is "yes."

I wish there was a way for us to measure soul sound. If we could hear the sounds of souls, wherever there is prayer—beneath and beyond the words—there would be cries. Cries of pain. Cries of grief. Cries of desperation. The cry may be the universal prayer. No eloquence, no great words, just the pure and woeful declaration of a soul apart from its source.

Will our cries be heard? Does sound travel far beyond the rope end? God will hear our cries, but often it seems the people around us don't. Everybody shows up for the funeral, and then they disappear after that. Often it can be chalked up to discomfort; family, friends, church members, even pastors frequently don't know what to say. So just when we are in the depths and feel far away from God and from others, the people around us keep their distance.

There we all are with a kind of spiritual separation anxiety attack. We have listened to sermons and prayers telling us God is right next to us, but we can't find him. We live and work next to people all the time but feel intensely alone. A child-rearing book assures parents whose children are experiencing separation anxiety, "A concentrated dose of mother and/or father love before you separate for the night can help make parting easier."[5] An extra dose of the Father's love before we separate would be great. An extra dose of a spouse's, friend's, or church member's love would help.

We all are crying out, in what feels like the dark, for our dead loved ones, for our pasts, for all that was once good. We are crying out just like when we were infants, not knowing if anyone—God or others—will come through that door.

## QUESTIONS

1. How have you experienced the death of loved ones?

2. What have you said when you have cried out to the Lord?

3. Can you recall the time or times when your crying out led to anger?

CHAPTER 5

WE ARE
# Angry

## Anger closes off the soul from God and others. It builds a wall around the soul.

"There is no greater obstacle to the presence
of the Spirit in us than anger."
—John Climacus

"Anger is the fever and frenzy of the soul."
—Thomas Fuller

Make a clenched fist and look at it. Somehow it looks angry, doesn't it? How is that? There are the white knuckles. It looks closed off, as if nothing can get in. We know that nothing good can come from a clenched fist. When a hand becomes a clenched fist it is to hurt or show anger toward someone.

It is no surprise that anger affects our bodies. According to a leading health website, a Johns Hopkins Medical School study confirms that young men who reacted to stress with anger were three times more likely to suffer from CHD (coronary heart disease) before the age of 55 than their peers who said they let stressful situations roll off their backs. In addition, other reports indicate that anger can cause arteries to narrow and constrict and platelets to stick together and cause blockages and cardiac arrests.[1] Other health reports in recent years have linked suppressed anger to high blood pressure and certain cancers.

Whether it is driving or angry confrontations on the little league field or at work and home, we appear to be angrier than ever. What are we so mad about? I think part of it is a sense of powerlessness. We live in a world that seems to be spinning increasingly out of control. Bystanders, we feel like we can't run on the field, so to speak, so we just become angrier and angrier.

One major source of powerlessness is faith. For a lot of reasons, we feel powerless to communicate with God, or get God's attention. And we hear all these great things about God, but many of us just don't see it. Our anger stems from feeling let down and betrayed and rejected. Just like in our human relationships, when we are rejected by loved ones or people we thought cared, after the hurt subsides, we often become very angry. When something to which we feel attached is taken away or changed, we may react with rage.

It may come as no surprise, for all the damage it does, that some scholars trace anger back to the beginning and heart of sin: "Anger has been rooted in the evil of humanness we express as resulting from 'the fall.' Anger must be seen, in the biblical vision, as rooted in creation."[2]

The misery that anger produces in homes and communities may not compare to what it does to the soul. If the clenched fist is an external sign of anger, imagine a soul looking like a clenched fist. "There is no greater obstacle to the presence of the Spirit in us than anger," wrote the sixth century scholarly monk, John Climacus. Anger closes off the soul from God and others. It builds a wall around the soul so that nothing can enter in. And nothing can leave.

The angry people I have known and tried to minister to have been very much like that. Their anger was so blinding—and often irrational—that it was difficult to reach them. In listening to the stories, so often a person consumed with anger has a long list of people who have wronged them.

At the top of the list many times is God, although anger at God is often suppressed. Somewhere along the way we are told that anger at God is inappropriate and wrong. It may be a distorted variation of "fearing the Lord." But if we are going to be in an authentic relationship with God, shouldn't all of our emotions be on the table?

As anger builds its wall tighter and tighter, it becomes "fevered and frenzied" because it is suffocating our souls. So much so that prayer and attending worship—nearly anything to do with God or his people—is gone. Our souls, which are designed to breathe by and with the Spirit of God, die a slow and painful death through anger; they are deprived of that which makes them live.

After years of barely breathing, our souls are compressed to virtually nothing. As our hands grip the end of our rope tighter and tighter, we notice how white our knuckles are and how our hands look like clenched fists. We think of our "mysterious" health problems that seem to flare up when we are angry. And it just makes us all the angrier thinking about how and why we are here.

## QUESTIONS

1. Do you feel like being angry has affected you or someone you know physically?

   If so, how?

2. Is there a connection between being angry and feeling powerless in life and in faith?

   Can you say more about that?

3. To deal with anger or other emotions, have you ever done things that seemed temporary at the time and now have become more permanent?

CHAPTER 6

## WE ARE
# Addicted

Everything that used to matter is ... eclipsed.

"Whatever man loves, that is his god.
For he carries it in his heart;
he goes about with it night and day;
he sleeps and wakes with it, be it what it may—
wealth or self, pleasure or renown."
—Martin Luther

There is something exciting and at the same time unsettling about an eclipse. The moon approaches the circle of the sun gradually. And then within moments the entire sun is covered except for the glow of the corona around the edges. The light of the sun is blocked out. As far as natural events, it is one of the most exciting to behold, but at the same time, there is that eerie light when the sun is fully eclipsed. Everything has this kind of yellow and gray look to it. It feels like things have changed—like another dimension or world has fallen upon us.

The interesting thing about a solar eclipse is that the sun, the light of this world and most of this galaxy, is blocked out basically by a rock that has no light of its own. But somehow, geometrically speaking, it seems to be able to obscure and darken the greatest light we know.

In our own lives, there are addictions that very gradually block our light—God—until he and most everything else looks and seems different to us. How and why we start down this road varies, but the end result is usually the same—everything that used to matter is eclipsed. The addictions themselves are not greater than God or loved ones or jobs, but as you know they have the power to obscure everything. And this kind of eclipse unfortunately lasts much longer than a few minutes.

"This time I am going to stop," Bill said confidently. It was the last time the drinking would go this far, he explained. It had been such a mess that it just had to stop.

But it wouldn't be the last time. And the reason that it wouldn't be the last time is because what perhaps Bill and millions of others have yet to realize is that his addiction had become his god. It was now something he needed—physically, mentally, and spiritually. It had gradually moved in front of God in his life until God was no longer visible in the same way.

Author Caroline Knapp captures this eclipse in her memoir, *Drinking: A Love Story*, when she writes, "Alcohol is everywhere in your life, omnipresent, and you're both aware and unaware of it almost all the time; all you know is that you would die without it, and there is no simple reason why this happens, no single moment, no physiological event that pushes a heavy drinker across a concrete line into alcoholism. It's a slow, gradual, insidious, elusive *becoming*."[1]

And here is the thing, when we make something a god in our lives that isn't God, it is the worst kind of deity—because it can only take, can accept worship but cannot redeem. It drains and sucks the life out of all of its worshippers until the souls and bodies are rotted away.

The sinister part of addictions, like an eclipse, is that it usually starts so small—just a piece of the sun is blocked. The drinking parties in middle school and high school seem harmless at the time—a rite of passage even.

Next, college life can become Functional Alcoholism 101. Then there is that point for so many when going out for drinks after work or fixing one each night is just a part of life. And then without even noticing, without warning, we *need* the drink. Up until this point it seemed like just the thing to do; and now it is *the* thing. Our bodies need the chemistry, our minds need the distraction, and our souls need the numbing. Without even noticing, we are at the end of a rope and that eerie yellow light colors everything we think and do. Other addictions follow the same pattern. Something else becomes that which centers us and affects our thoughts and actions—perhaps the role God used to play.

Addictions, for most, are secret loves. We keep them hidden from family members, spouses, church members, and ministers. And in some ways, churches—in an effort to not offend—can unintentionally maintain the façade. I think churches and ministers would be very surprised at how many of their members appear to be listening to the sermon or homily but are actually thinking about when the service is going to end so that they can get home and have a drink or a pill or download another picture.

It must be so hard to look around a sanctuary and think that all the other people don't have problems and aren't wrestling with this need. I think this is why many addicted people don't come to church anymore; to feel like you are the only broken one is a lonely feeling.

However we reach the end of our rope, in this case through addictions, we very often feel like the only ones who have problems. The spiritual part of it is that we feel like God wants us to use the back door, too—if that. And we have this sneaking suspicion that something is not right—this kind of eclipse coloring of life. Our relationships are failing, motivation is gone, we have lost jobs because of our addictions and yet somehow we are blind to the fact that whatever is eclipsing God in our lives is the problem.

On some level, many of us know that the drinking and the pills and the pot and the porn are harmful and damaging. But the end of the rope is a place where even if we know, we can't do anything about it, or no longer have the will to.

Just like with an eclipse, there is still light. It's not like it is night, and we know the difference. You can still see, but everything has changed. And every once in a while, we wonder if the true light will break through again sometime, someday.

## QUESTIONS

1. After reading this chapter, is there anything harmful that has become such a presence in your life that you couldn't live without it?

2. Can you sense a loss of will or motivation in areas of your life because something that only drains you has become your center?

3. With this "thing" at your center, does it leave you afraid at times for what is happening?

# CHAPTER 7

## WE ARE
# Afraid

Fear is part of what keeps us from believing there is such a thing as a second chance.

> "No passion so effectively robs the mind of all its powers of acting and reasoning as fear."
> —Edmund Burke

We don't really think about gravity too much. It's there, it's working—that's it. We seem only to notice it when we fall or when the plane is taking off. But we never really think about how it is constantly pulling us down, holding us on the earth.

Fear is kind of like that. It is always there, working most of the time without us noticing. It is only when we approach something new, or something from our past, or something challenging that we feel the pull. It is like the plane taking off. On the runway, we don't feel anything different. It is only when the plane takes off that moment when the thrust of the plane overcomes the pull of gravity. That is when we feel the pull.

The thing about gravity is that it always just pulls one way—down. But fear pulls in all sorts of directions. It is often why once we get to the end of our rope, it is very difficult to move. Physics is hard enough. The physics of faith are even more complicated.

Not as complicated is how children deal with fears. They're afraid of monsters, loud noises, the dark, being away from parents, and not knowing what to do in new situations. Somehow we aren't much different. Only the contexts have changed. The playground becomes the conference room; the batter's box becomes the podium during a presentation. The friend moving away becomes the waiting for the phone call in the middle of the night. The pull of fear remains the same while the consequences mean more.

Although, fear seems to become more polarizing when we are adults. For example, we are afraid to succeed, and we are afraid to fail. We are afraid of what we want but are afraid to be without it and afraid to ask for it. We fear giving our whole selves to someone in love because we fear being rejected. The goal of the Enemy is achieved—we stay stuck.

We do this with God, too. We fear that God is real and we fear that God is not real. On one hand, we fear that God is real because of what it would mean to our lives; all the implications and possibilities are and can be overwhelming. It is the "too good to be true" principle. And so as much as we want to believe it, we convince ourselves that it can't be true. On the other hand, we also fear that there is no God. This would mean that we have all been fooled—that this has all been a scam. The stories, the years of trying to believe and hope in something we cannot see, the skepticism of friends would all come back on us—someone somewhere would be laughing at us. Nobody wants to be a fool and so the fear keeps us believing just a little bit. If we only believe a little bit, either way—real or not real—we are covered.

But we don't just fear God himself. The fear affects how we live out our faith. We even come to fear the possibility of fully following Jesus. We fear this because, if true, it would be radical—a radically different and new way of living—

totally outside of this balance. And then we also have come to fear (and rightly) the judgment and treatment of people in churches.

Is it any wonder that many times when a person in the Bible is approached by an angel or messenger or even Jesus himself, they start with the requisite "Be not afraid."?

Fear has a devastating effect on faith—in part because it is its near opposite. Fear is part of what keeps us from believing there is such a thing as a second chance, as well as that we can have one. It is what makes us deny that God loves us and what keeps us from pursuing God with reckless abandon.

We also feel this fear force when we try to draw nearer to others. We can literally feel it pulling us away from the new friend or the person to whom we would like to introduce ourselves. It's that voice that says, "They don't want to talk to you," or "When they get to know the real you, they will be repulsed."

At the same time fear has this effect where after the pull wears off, after we have approached defying gravity or doubt or the past, and pulled back, we feel better. We are not any safer or more secure or closer to answers, but the stomach turning feeling of the pull has gone away. And in the end, that is what we want to avoid, right? Fear is that force (in a twisted way) that helps achieve equilibrium. The thinking is that nature and people want to have stability and balance (for better or worse) that enables a kind of equilibrium.

The irony of course is that the very equilibrium we seek can be as isolating and trying as the end of our rope. So fear is that force that is keeping us stuck here at the end of our rope as much as it drove us here in the first place. We become afraid to move up, afraid to move further down, and afraid to let go. But at least we don't feel the pull anymore.

## QUESTIONS

1. Can you think of specific areas of your life in which you can feel fear pulling or holding you down?

2. Which is scarier—God being real or God being make believe?

   Can you share why?

3. Do you ever fear that there is nothing on this earth that will fulfill your life?

CHAPTER 8

## WE ARE
# Unfulfilled

There is no fast food for the soul.

In homes across the nation, late at night, you can see the flickering light of the televisions in darkened living rooms and bedrooms. It is the "light" of the infomercials streaming into our lives. You know, the infomercial—the thirty- or sixty-minute commercial that through cheesy spokespeople and bizarre audience participation, persuades viewers to buy things. Clearly, infomercials and the products they push are an indication of who we are and where we are. According to infomercials, all we want are cooking products, sex videos, exercise machines, and to get rich. Maybe that *is* all that we want anymore.

And yet, they do reveal something about our wants and desires. They, like most other marketing, confirm that we all have this innate hunger for something. Although, instead of food processors, videos, and real estate programs, if we broke down all of our wants they would actually be some or all of these: security, peace, to be loved and accepted, to feel empowered and significant. Please know there is nothing wrong with wanting these things—on their own they are good. And you know these are not just things that we want passively. Quite the opposite; for better or for worse, for life or destruction, we are very passionate about pursuing these things. For many of us it literally drives us. By the way, all of these things and more flow abundantly from a personal relationship with God (that is the design) but that takes faith.

And so here we are growing up with this hunger, this Grand Canyon of thirst, that acts as a kind of a vacuum (by design to be filled with and by God). In the absence or avoidance of God though, other things fill our souls.

Look all around us: From our homes, to the grocery store to television and the internet—all around are these invitations to want and get more, to fill the emptiness.

Think of all the attics and storage closets and self-storage places sprouting up all over the place, crammed for the most part with things that don't matter. According to industry statistics, the number of U.S. households that now rent a self-storage unit has increased 50 percent over the last ten years; and there is 17.2 square feet of self storage inventory per household.[1] How can we have all of this stuff and space for stuff and still feel empty as individuals and as a people?

This "wanting it all" burns within us for different reasons. Perhaps it is because we were deprived of love and nurturing as children and now we will do almost anything to have love and keep it. Maybe we grew up with little and we became convinced that the answer to the problems of the past was to have more money and things. Whatever our void was or is, it certainly seems to help determine what we hunger for and what we do to satisfy the urge.

One of the signature film and cultural influences of the last thirty years, *Star Wars*, is essentially about the redemption of a man, Anakin Skywalker/Darth Vader, who desires to be the most powerful Jedi (he already is). He has an insatiable desire for power and control. How did it all start for Anakin? Repeatedly in the films he makes reference to how losing his mother as a young man drove him to want to have the power to control life—at all costs—so that he would never lose anyone again. And in his quest for this power he ends up killing the woman he loved, nearly killing his best friend, and being consumed physically and spiritually by the power he sought.

It may be science fiction, but it is played out in the real world everyday. Husbands and wives crave more attention and more success and they are consumed by affairs and jobs and their lives are wrecked. Families stretch their finances for the best homes and cars and are consumed and owned by debt.

Part of it is that we believe or convince ourselves that happiness as it has been defined for us is just around the corner. That with the better job, the better cell phone, the bigger house, or a different spouse, life would be okay— better than okay, fixed; it would be satisfying. People say things like, "I just want you to be happy." Of course it is meant well. But happiness is so fleeting and hard to define that it falls very short of the thing God offers to us—peace.

In the absence of God, we sometimes turn to substances that offer a temporary *feeling* of peacefulness. If we are dying to be loved and accepted and don't experience that from the Lord, from a church or others, we often mold ourselves into something else and connect with people who will accept us. Along the same lines, many of us choose the path of behaving in ways we know are not God's and are destructive just to *feel* loved. We have all done something that we later regret just to be loved.

Our desire and our passion is God-designed and given to us for a specific purpose—to hunger for that which pleases God and the soul. But, as humans, we have warped and twisted our desires and passions to serve another purpose: ourselves—our immediate needs. Let's be honest, you have noticed pleasing God seems complicated (or has been made confusing by churches and others) and pleasing the soul, well, that just takes time. There is no fast food for the soul.

I can't tell you when it starts to go awry because I am not sure. Maybe it begins for us as children with toys. Perhaps it starts to build for us as teenagers with friends. But by the time we are all adults, it has taken hold and it is a battle to the end. And it is most likely the main reason many of us are at the end of our ropes.

This insatiable, unstoppable desire for more, better, and bigger seems to have infected every aspect of life, and it shows no sign of stopping no matter what the consequences are.

How much pain and wreckage have come from our warped desires, our desperate attempts to satisfy ourselves?

How many marriages, families, and businesses are wrecked every day because of our hunger for more or for better? You may be sitting in that kind of wreckage right now. Because the answer to everything—the emptiness, the void, the nothingness—is just one purchase, one meal, one affair away. And the thing that just doesn't make sense is that no matter how many times we hunger and thirst and want and take, it always is still just one step more away. It stays just out of reach.

If we were to do a survey, few of us would be able to clearly articulate exactly for what we are hungering. When we are at the end of our rope, words like meaning, purpose, and fulfillment seem ludicrous. We might say we want power to feel in control. How shocking it must be when we realize that the more we accumulate and stockpile, the more the emptiness and lack of power grows? What kind of strange algebra is this?

Jesus once said, "For what will it profit them if they gain the whole world but forfeit their life? (Matthew 16:26). We are fulfilling his words today like never before. We have gained the whole world in nearly every way. But we also know that we have forfeited life—living—as it was intended. The life of the soul has virtually been lost; worse than lost—clicked off because there had to be something else more exciting.

And as the television flickers in our homes at night and the infomercials run continuously, all we know is that we just want more. Here at the end of the rope we are starving and thirsting for things that have no names and no value. We want them so bad it hurts; we feel like we won't be able to live without them. And yet, we can't even tell you what exactly they are. We just want more of them. More attention, more money, more stuff, it just doesn't ever stop because the emptiness never seems to fill up. We reach and grasp despite the fact that there never was, never is, and never will be enough.

## QUESTIONS

1. Think of your home or storage space; how much of the "stuff" is important?

   Has having all this "stuff" ever satisfied you in a meaningful way?


2. Do you have it "all" but still feel like you have nothing?

   Can you explore that?


3. Can you detect nothingness or decaying within your soul?

   If so, for how long have you felt it?

CHAPTER 9

WE ARE

# Sinful

We are trapped between rehearsed, inauthentic
confessions or the fear of judgment and
ostracism from sharing with others.

"We are as sick as our secrets."
—Anonymous

Can you feel it?

Different poisons and toxins work in different ways. Some
quickly affect the central nervous system or the digestive
system. Some work slower over time and deteriorate bones,
organs, and other body functions. The results can range
from a rash to seizures to death. It all depends on the
amount consumed, the level of toxicity of the poison and
the amount of time it stays in our bodies.

According to some sources, there are about 10 million
poisonings each year in the United States. And yet, while
dictionaries and medical books may not talk about it, there
is another more pervasive poisoning problem in our lives.
Listen to this ancient poison report from the Bible: "There
is no soundness in my flesh because of your indignation;
there is no health in my bones because of my sin. For my
iniquities have gone over my head; they weigh like a burden
too heavy for me" (Psalm 38:3–4).

They didn't have any poison control centers back then. But they understood, as we do now, the connection between the health of the soul and body and mind. When we experience a kind of physical or chemical poisoning, you know what it does to us. It is distracting and annoying and uncomfortable and sickening. But what about soul poisoning? Just like this passage describes, the things that are corroding our souls translate into physical responses such as "no soundness in my flesh" and "no health in my bones." The voice of these words is falling apart. Then and now, it is part of what it feels like to be at the end of the rope.

Do you recall that the universal symbol of a poison or toxic substance is the skull and crossbones? It makes sense doesn't it? If there are things that are destroying our souls and consequently our bodies, then all that will be left will be bones. And that is what many believers and churches feel like—like dried up bones (Ezekiel 37:11). You see, our souls can be and are poisoned. It's sin and guilt that "destroy and impair" that health of our souls. You know that sin is disregarding and disobeying God's ways. Its toxic partner, guilt, is also a destroyer of souls, bodies, and lives in that over time it breaks down our God-given buoyancy.

When it comes to sin, it seems that so many of us have been affected by poor teaching. We have such a distorted view of what sin really is and how we are to deal with it. So many people have stories of being told that their sins are beyond God's ability to forgive; that the amount of time they have spent away from God and church has been too long; that the distance their souls have gone from the Lord is too far. After a while, when you are condemned over and over again by a person of authority, it starts to stick.

Now it is true that sin is deadly and has disabled our ability to follow God on our own. But the other half of the message about sinfulness is that with God's help, the deadliness and destruction of sin can be overcome. Are we sinful? Yes. Are we any less children of God because of sin? Not according to God. "Sinner" should not be a slur—especially since it describes all of us.

The other poor teaching is that sin is not a problem at all. This is as much dishonest as it is naïve. The message that virtually nothing that we do or say needs to be forgiven is also a misunderstanding of God's grace. Sin is for real and causes untold damage to our lives. So when people are taught not to worry about it, this makes it worse. When someone is poisoned with strychnine, we don't just ignore it and hope it goes away.

And just like with poisons and toxins, it is not only their lethality that matters; their impact also has to do with how long they are in our system. In spiritual terms, this is what guilt is to the soul. It acts as an agent that keeps sins forgiven and unforgiven in the soul. It acts like platelets to blood. Guilt acts as a seal around the soul that keeps the poison inside. Guilt is this build-up of sins—years and thousands of sins that then cloud who we are in God's eyes. Of course there is healthy guilt—when we do something wrong, we regret it and feel responsible. But then there is guilt that we feel responsible for things that we haven't even done or have already been forgiven or taken care of. What is the combined weight of years of sins and guilt and feelings of failure that we carry around? For many, it feels like tons.

Tragically, toxic guilt has often been injected into us by the very institution that should be offering the antidote— the church. For many reasons, guilt has been spread by churches through poor teaching and as a means of control.

Part of why we feel we have thousands of pounds and years of sins bottled up inside of us poisoning our souls and bodies is because we don't have a safe place to expel them. In other words, from whatever Christian tradition you may come, there is an understanding of confessing sins. But it is such that we are trapped between rehearsed, inauthentic confessions or the fear of judgment and ostracism from sharing with others. There is always the route of giving our sins and guilt to the Lord, but in our poisoned state we often either don't want to face him or believe that he will not forgive.

Another ancient voice describes this experience today, "While I kept silence (about my sins), my body wasted away through my groaning all day long. For day and night your hand was heavy upon me; my strength was dried up as by the heat of summer" (Psalm 32:3–4). If possible, when sins become secrets, when we keep them to ourselves, their deadliness is enhanced because they become more attached to our souls—glued by guilt.

So we have millions of God's children poisoned, suffering and dying in silence much more than they would be naturally because of all of this. Millions of God's children are falling apart because their "soundness of the flesh and bones" is failing.

Can you feel it?

We weren't designed for sin. But it is here, and there is something we can do about it. We weren't designed to carry the guilt and weight of all of our sins—someone else took care of that. But we are doing it anyway. We weren't designed to hang perilously from the ends of our ropes. But here we are.

We are living as if the poison has already finished its work, living like we are just bones—dried up, brittle, silent, and lifeless.

## QUESTIONS

1. What are the secrets that you are keeping inside and that may be poisoning you from the inside out?

2. How toxic are your body and soul at this point?

   How about other parts of your life—like relationships, and sense of purpose or meaning?

3. Meanwhile, as awful as you may feel, how does being judged for all of it make you feel?

## CHAPTER 10

WE ARE

# Judged

## To be told that you are not good enough for God ... this is to be judged.

"Most of us are umpires at heart;
we like to call balls and strikes on somebody else."
—Leo Aikman

Remember how our parents used to measure our height with little pencil marks on a wall? That was just the introduction to this world of measuring us. The voices of parents, siblings, teachers, ministers, and others along the way begin to build and shape a whole system of measuring our lives against the monolithic standard of "enough." So that the innocence of "How tall am I?" eventually and sadly becomes the obsessive "Am I good enough?"

We are constantly being measured and judged against varying standards of "enough." There are the surface things like hair, clothes, and beauty. Then there are the measurements of wealth and success such as cars, homes, job titles, and portfolios. We are judged by how successful our children are at school and sports. And we are measured by our personal conduct.

In part, we are driven to succeed on the world's terms to avoid being judged or measured. Let's face it, if you have all the right stuff and look good, you are pretty much not

judged in a traditional sense. We might call it judgment
prevention.

Growing up, we had very little money. We lived in a
two-bedroom apartment, often needed financial help
from other family members, and for many years couldn't
afford to go on vacations. And yet, I remember my mother
spending a lot of time and money (that we didn't have) on
making sure my brother and I had "nice" outfits. Today,
I understand that her thinking was that if we looked
presentable, we might be able to distract people from the
truth of our circumstances—to delay the judgment.

In truth, who are the people who get judged and
measured the most? In our society, it is the people who are
most in need, hurting the most because they don't measure
up. The poor, the disabled, single parents, and many others
are judged.

There is this great children's book by Max Lucado called,
*You Are Special.* The story is about these wooden people made
uniquely but equal by a master woodcarver. These wooden
people go around and give each other stars if they look
great or do talented things and gray dots if they are silly and
foolish. The main character, Punchinello, is someone who
constantly gets gray dots and he feels awful about himself.
At one point in the book, others give him gray dots because
he already has so many.

Isn't this what we do? We often tell the pregnant
unmarried couple or the single pregnant woman, who may
already feel bad, to get out. Many times, we tell divorced
couples that they failed and make sure it is uncomfortable
for one or both of them. We let the depressed and the
alcoholics know that they are miserable disappointments.
They and their conduct just don't measure up; they will
never be good enough or holy enough. Sometimes people
who don't have money for nice clothes are made to feel
inadequate at church because they aren't dressed up to

code. One way or another, we let sinners know that their kind isn't welcome.

To be told that you are not good enough for God; that you are not worthy to come to church; that you are too sinful to gather with other believers—this is to be judged. To feel like you are unworthy has to be one of the worst human experiences. To be named unworthy by someone else is to be excluded, cast out. Jesus cast out demons, not sinners. It must feel so dreadful to be told by other believers that you are beyond God's reach.

How does it feel for others, not God, to make that determination for you? It must feel desperate and sickening to think that God (through his spokespeople) has cast you out and condemned you. Oh, the damage that is done when we step in and try to do what is clearly God's work. We can try to rationalize and say things like, "Judgments from other people should just be shrugged off." Is that really the case when it comes to things like the worth of our souls and eternal life?

Over the years, so many people have said to me after I have invited them to church, "Oh, you don't want me there. The roof will cave in." You might have thought this yourself. Where did this thinking come from? Should only "good" or "holy" people go to church? The "bad" or "sinful" people should stay home?

A colleague once asked some people at one of my churches, "You know what a sinner is?" He paused and scanned the perplexed faces as they braced for the usual list of choices and behaviors. "A sinner is someone in need of God's grace," he said, surprising them all.

God knows we are sinners. And we know we are sinners for whom a debt has already been paid. So why do we have all of this reminding from other sinners about how sinful we are? Judgment is when we apply human measurements to that which is eternal. We are so obsessed with measuring and counting that we count sins, too. But it is deeper than that. Judgment often serves a community purpose. Judgment pushes away, judgment hurts, judgment keeps believers safe from "those people"—judgment keeps others at a distance.

And yet, who was Jesus always being accused of hanging around with? Sinners—though their lives were being transformed by his presence. How can we be transformed by his presence if we believe or have been told we aren't good enough to be near him or his people?

At the same time, we have become much shrewder about applying judgment today. We may no longer throw stones, but we haven't stopped taking shots. Instead, it can just be a casual comment or the frown down the pew or in the grocery store to remind us how repulsive we are and how we really are unworthy. Ignoring is also a stealth judgment tool. It goes back to the surface or image—we don't want to appear that we are judging. It would be terrible if people thought we were judgmental. So we will just be a little more subversive about it.

What does all this overt and covert judging accomplish? We have a society intensely driven to control appearance and image, virtually abandoning soul and substance. We have a cultural mindset that programs nearly everyone that they are not and never will be good enough for God and for the rest of us. We have congregations either being poorly taught or are so deep in denial about sin that they are using judgment to protect themselves from the "unholy" people. The result of all of this is that we have thousands of churches struggling just to keep their doors open and millions of believers alienated from God and many more millions confused by the gracelessness of it all. But who's counting?

## QUESTIONS

1.  How does it feel when you don't measure up?

2.  Have you been made to feel that you are not "good enough" for God?

    What was that like?

3.  Doesn't the judging and trying to avoid being judged make you feel trapped and imprisoned?

    Can you think of some words that describe this experience?

CHAPTER 11

WE ARE
# Depressed

When prisoners, chained in despair, break down
and resolve that they are no longer redeemable.

> "In a real dark night of the soul it is always
> three o'clock in the morning."
>
> —F. Scott Fitzgerald
> *The Crack-Up*

If the hiding and the darkness has the feel or illusion of a
choice, there is a place beyond it—the prison of the soul.
The prison has no key because it has no door. We cannot
escape because it is within—it's our soul that becomes a
prison. And when a soul becomes a prison, it may be the
most unnatural thing ever. It is the very bottom of the end
of the rope.

Depression is a spiritual condition too. No matter how or
why one has reached this level of despair—it is a spiritual
prison. First, you know that the alive spiritual life is one in
which affection is given and received—from God and from
others. If that function were to be suspended by depression
and other forces, the spiritual life would cease as well.

A sense of purpose evaporates in the prison of the soul.
When we are in this depth of despair, we just don't see any
purpose to our lives. It seems that God has made a mistake
in putting us on the earth. Our sense of value is eliminated.
We just feel worthless—that there is nothing of value that

we have done or represent. Our ability to love is removed. It is one of those things where we can reason that we might be loved or that we in concept love others but we can't feel it anymore. Our desire to live is drained from us. When we are at this point, we are bored by the things we used to love. We just don't feel like participating in life anymore. There is a fatigue that comes with depression that seems strange when we aren't even able to exert ourselves. Everything feels like drudgery. Even to cry out and pray seems futile. Our power to grow is unplugged in this soul prison. We don't have any incentive to grow anymore in this state. Growth would probably mean more energy and more pain. So the best we can do is just hold up where we are and try to get through. All hope, all dreams, all loves are cut off. There is no bottom, there is no top, there is no beginning and no end; there just is, and when you are depressed even that doesn't matter.

This is what a prison of the soul is like. All of these things: purpose, value, loving, living, growth—all the things that God either gives to us or wants for us—are slowly and painfully destroyed. It is a soul death sentence.

A result of all of this is the distortion of vision and reality. Even in the early stages of depression this distortion is evident, and it worsens as the condition deepens. Experiencing this level of despair, being this far down the rope literally affects the way we see reality, God, and others.

Listen to this voice of despair: "He has made my flesh and my skin waste away, and broken my bones; he has besieged me and enveloped me with bitterness and tribulation; he has made me sit in darkness like the dead of long ago. He has walled me about so that I cannot escape; he has put heavy chains on me" (Lamentations 3:4–7).

The "he" in these verses from the book of Lamentations is God. While this passage truly captures what it feels like to be depressed, it also illustrates the kind of distortion that occurs when we begin to think that the Lord is the warden of our prison. You know that this is not what God wants for us.

The tragic part of depression and despair is that we are often surrounded by people who only want to help us and care for us, even rescue us. But this distortion is powerful in that friends and loved ones seem like enemies. We stretch out our hands from behind the prison bars because friends and family appear to be right outside—within reach so much so that we could touch them—but we can never reach them.

I heard a story about a guy who committed suicide. His death was as tragic as all suicides are. But the circumstances prior to taking his life are—if possible—more stunning. The night before he killed himself, he attended a Bible study at his church. From all indications, no one reported anything out of the ordinary. People knew that he was under a lot of stress. But it must have been so sad for him to have sat at the Bible study, listening and learning about the hope of the Gospel but unable to ask for help.

In the cold, and the isolation and the distortion of the soul prison, a kind of death comes. It begins when a prisoner, chained in despair, breaks down and resolves that he or she is no longer redeemable, nor lovable, nor worth rescuing.

Elizabeth Wurtzel captures this declaration in her memoir *Prozac Nation: Young and Depressed in America,* "No one will ever love me, I will live and die alone, I will go nowhere fast, I will be nothing at all. Nothing will work out. The promise that on the other side of depression lies a beautiful life, one worth surviving suicide for, will have turned out wrong. It will all be a big dupe."[1]

The prison of a soul is the most unnatural place ever because it is the absolute converse of the design of a human life and existence. And for millions it is all too real, even though you couldn't find it on a map. You can't tell anyone what it looks like or what color it is. You only know it because it has a pain that doesn't hurt, sorrow without tears, breathing without air, walking without moving, living without being alive, faith without believing, and answers without questions.

## QUESTIONS

1.  Do you struggle with giving and receiving affection?

    How does that play out in your life?


2.  Do you feel like you are imprisoned and that God is the warden?


3.  Are you surrounded by people who can't help?

    Can you share what that is like?

## CHAPTER 12

WE ARE

# Disenchanted

### Few things make sense anymore.

> "Doubt isn't the opposite of faith;
> it is an element of faith."
>
> —Paul Tillich

You have heard of the five W's right? You know—Who, What, When, Where, and Why.

Have you ever thought of the vast difference between the first four and the last one? For an event or story most people can figure out the Who, the What, the When, and the Where. But then there is the Why. It is so vastly different that it almost doesn't belong with the others.

For example, you could have been crossing Hudson Place to reach your usual entrance steps leading to the PATH commuter trains on September 11, 2001, at 8:45 a.m. (late again) and when you glanced up quickly over at the World Trade Center towers and you caught a glimpse of a commercial jet flying south and unusually low over lower Manhattan. This covers the Who, What, When and Where.

But when you looked again, stopped everything—motion, breath, thought—and tracked the plane as it pierced the glass and steel of the North Tower, all the other questions fall short. What's left has a chance of beginning to deal with the inexplicable—"Why?"

Though you may not have known it at the time, you have also asked "why" racing through the automatic doors of the emergency room; driving to the cemetery; defending yourself from your husband; cleaning out your desk and walking out the door escorted by security.

You see, the first four W's are questions of the mind; they have to do with facts. "Why" is a question that is for, and comes from, the soul.

As humans, there is a part of us that desires meaning and reasons and explanations for things that happen. This thirst for meaning is continuous, and it increases during seemingly senseless times. Have you noticed that few things make sense anymore? What was taken for granted is now gone, what worked before is now obsolete, what was believable is now a lie, what was important is now trivial, and what was thriving is now dead. You are at the rope's end.

A sustained time at the end of our rope is often accompanied by excruciating meaninglessness. And this is why "Why?" is much more than a standard inquiry. You understand that the purpose of asking questions is to ascertain truth or gain information or increase awareness.

Pastors and churchgoers so often feel like they must have an answer—even when there just isn't one. "It was God's will," people frequently assure others and themselves. It may be God's will, but that doesn't help answer the question and it doesn't make anybody feel better! I think part of it may stem from the fear that if one doesn't have an answer—it might reflect poorly on his or her faith—either in terms of knowledge or belief. It is as if having questions and doubts threaten faith, so the approach is avoid and deny and minimize—rather than listen and embrace. Often, we have sought comfort and wisdom from churches and pastors, only to leave with more "whys" than when we arrived.

Perhaps, the not so obvious reason behind asking the question "why" has to do with relationship. Asking "why" has something behind it. It suggests connection. We don't ask strangers "why" with any real intention. "Why" in the form of a prayer or a cry says, "Why would you (God) let this happen?" Could "why" be the first word of the majority of prayers to God? "I loathe my life; I will give free utterance to my complaint; I will speak in the bitterness of my soul. I will say to God, Do not condemn me; let me know why you contend against me," says Job in the Bible (Job 10:1–2).

Job, as you may know, lost everything—his children were killed; his wife left him; he lost his health, his property, his animals—he was stripped. It is the ultimate worst case scenario.

But Job never curses the Lord. It would be difficult to even say that he blames God. But he does hold God responsible, not so much for the events, but for the implications for his relationship with the Lord. Chapter 10 of the book of Job presents many "why" oriented prayers and questions. What follows are the original verses from Job 10 followed by my translated version (in italics) of what Job is saying to God:

3 Does it please you to oppress me, to spurn the work of your hands, while you smile on the schemes of the wicked?

*Why do you enjoy watching good people suffer?*

8 "Your hands shaped me and made me.
Will you now turn and destroy me?
9 Remember that you molded me like clay.
Will you now turn me to dust again?
10 Did you not pour me out like milk
and curdle me like cheese,

*You made me and then you destroy me, what is up with that?*

13 "But this is what you concealed in your heart,
and I know that this was in your mind:

*You have been good to me, so why were you*
*just waiting to take it all away?*

15 If I am guilty—woe to me! Even if I am innocent,
I cannot lift my head, for I am full of shame
and drowned in [a] my affliction.
16 If I hold my head high, you stalk me like a lion
and again display your awesome power against me.
17 You bring new witnesses against me
and increase your anger toward me;
your forces come against me wave upon wave.

*Why are you out to get me? What did I do?*

20 Are not my few days almost over?
Turn away from me so I can have a moment's joy
21 before I go to the place of no return,
to the land of gloom and deep shadow, [a]
22 to the land of deepest night, of deep shadow and
disorder, where even the light is like darkness."

*This is not going to end well.*
*There is no light at the end of the tunnel.*

Today, we might have some similar questions for God:

*Why do you let children get slaughtered and*
*molested in this world?*

*I go to church and worship you and then I lose my job? Why?*
*Why are you out to get me? What did I do?*

*Why did you let these things (abuse, neglect, disease)*
*happen to me?*

There is no official language of the end of our rope. But the most commonly used word is "why." "Why" might be the closest thing to a knot to grab onto on the rope here; though as you have already noticed you can't get a good grip. "Why" is the only thing that makes sense to ask or say or pray in a place that has lost all sense.

The prayer of "Why" defiantly insists there must be meaning and that there must be a relationship, God's relationship with people, to be held accountable.

Job, in the face of all of his losses—when his life has lost all meaning—asked the Lord "Why?" And while he never received a full answer he did receive a terrifying but transforming conversation with God. All that he lost came back to him twofold (Job 42).

Yet "Why?" remains the hardest question to ask and the most difficult to hear the answer to. There often is no direct answer to this question, but there is always a response. Your arrival and long stay here at the end of the rope has always been incomprehensible. You have been left hanging and swinging by the people and places you thought were there to reach out to you. You have gone over it so many times and still all you can come up with are the Who, What, When and Where. But maybe there is one more prayer in your soul.

## QUESTIONS

1. Do you find yourself asking God, "Why?" a lot?

   When you do, what are the "Whys" about?

2. Why would God let all this happen to us and to this world?

   Can you share some thoughts about this?

3. What is that one prayer left in your soul?

## Part Two

## GOD IS ... ILLUMINATED

If there is one prayer in our souls, it might be something like this: "Lord, I need to know you are real, right now!"

The rope end is distorting, like one of those mirrors at a fun house. Nothing looks right—ourselves, others, circumstances, or even God. At the same time, there's a certain clarity at the end of the rope. Sure, part of it is desperation. We have nothing left to lose or nothing better to do, so we take a closer look and we are more open to seeing things we didn't want to before. But it also comes out of a need; we reach a point where, unlike ever before, we need to see God—who he really is, if he is all he claims to be. For a long time, we've thought God isn't all that we were told. This is the God from whom we walked away.

But at this point we don't need a public relations photo of God or Sunday school propaganda. We need to see the heart of God. We need to see what God is made of. If not now, then when?

What is in God's heart? We can never fully know; it is beyond comprehension. But we do have some clues. Clues, it turns out, which we may have seen before.

The memories of hearing about purpose, grace, and community and of valuing each one of us haven't faded completely. There are the glimpses of miracles, wonders, and of beautiful things beyond eyesight.

It's like the shoebox of old, faded Polaroids we have stored deep in a closet. We know we want to look at them, but we also know that it will be heartbreaking. We know where to look though, if we ever want to go there. But if we were to dump them out and arrange them just right we might be able to see a bigger, clearer picture.

Maybe we would see a master craftsman bent on purposefully breaking through the old, the broken, and the silence to sculpt something new. Perhaps we would rediscover a shepherd intent on finding the lost and bringing them home. Possibly, we would perceive a savior all about standing between us and judgment. Conceivably, we might make out a father set on loving us and valuing things that we can barely recognize in our world today. Altogether, this composite would show a God who has designed and built within the faith a structure and method of starting over.

It looks like the God of whom we have dreamed and heard about as children, the same one who has been fuzzy and unclear since then. This is the God we glimpsed and convinced ourselves it couldn't be true.

It is like staying awake and watching a sunrise after a long, stormy, prayerful night—like seeing a sunrise, which happens everyday, as if it were new and at the same time— just as glorious and marvelous as we remember it.

## CHAPTER 13

## GOD IS

# Patient

"Yet even now ..."

"For everything there is a season,
and a time for every matter under heaven"
—Ecclesiastes 3:1

We are always running late. We're late for work, late to pick up the kids; dinner is late, bills are late, bedtime is late. It seems like that is just the accepted way. Is there such a thing as "too late"?

Actually, I guess we can be too late with a bunch of things. The bills can only be late so many times without affecting our credit score. We can only be late to work so many times before being written up or fired. Lateness takes its toll on our minds and bodies.

When we start to believe that it has become too late for ourselves, we are at the end of our rope. There is something that happens at the end of our rope through which we can become convinced that we will not be recognized or remembered by God and by others. It is a slow-growing belief that overcomes us. But it grows to the point where we just stop looking in the mirror, stop praying, stop hoping. "God's doesn't know me anymore," we think. We believe that we have become beyond recognition.

I have seen this in the eyes of many people. I catch it as they look down and away while I greet them. The sad part is that I recognize them, but they can't see that anymore.

We also think that with all the poison of sin and guilt flowing through our bodies, it has become too late to save us. As with recognition, this too is a slow but inevitable death. And there just doesn't seem to be anything to stop it. The corruption has exceeded the redemption threshold.

I have heard the stories of many people who are convinced that all the things they have done have disqualified them with God. I wish I had a nickel for each time I invited someone to church and they said to me, "You don't want the roof to cave in, do you?" By the way, to date, a sinner entering a church has not caused a roof collapse.

As we become accustomed to that weird eclipse light, it also dawns on us that it might be too late to keep it from being permanent. We may not admit it, but we know that it feels like it is too late when we have become prisoners and slaves to work, alcohol and drugs, and porn. *This eclipse is never going to end; the real light is not coming back*, we think.

I have sat in bars and living rooms with people who may not say it with words, but somehow speak volumes about how it was too late. With each drink, they slip further and further away. They're not happy about it; there is no rejoicing. But they would tell me that there is nothing that can be done. It is a sort of distorted surrender after which the war continues on anyway.

Perhaps the worst feeling, though, is when we feel stuck in the prison inside. Just being in there is bad enough. The inner prison of despair is designed to lead you to believe that it is too late to expect anyone to come and break you out. And as the flame of hope and desire to leave slowly fades, we just come around to the conviction that we are beyond rescue.

The most heartbreaking conversations have been the ones with brothers and sisters who have convinced themselves that their lives are not worth the effort. There is nothing for me to say. But to sit across from a child of God who thinks they are beyond reach and redemption is one of the hardest things to do as a pastor and a brother. I know what I want to say; I know the answer but I also know that it would be a drop in the ocean. That's not to say I don't say anything, but I see the reality of the prison inside. And of course there are many who can't or won't even have that conversation; and I understand that too. But if I ever get the chance, here is what I would say to him or her. First, I would say that I loved them; that is why I keep praying, reaching out, calling, and writing. And I would add that I care very much about how they are at the end of their rope; that it breaks my heart and I want to make it go away. And that it doesn't matter to me how they got there. Then I would say God loves them too. I would say that God loves them in a way that is unlike anything else. I would add that God loves them so much that as long as they have breath, it is never too late to come back to him. "Yet even now, says the Lord, return to me with all your heart, with fasting, with weeping, and with mourning; rend your hearts and not your clothing. Return to the Lord, your God, for he is gracious and merciful and slow to anger, and abounding in steadfast love, and relents from punishing" (Joel 2:12–13).

"Yet even now ...," says to me that no matter how many sins or failures—no matter how years or miles we have gone—as long as we are still alive, we can come back home by "rending" our hearts in Jesus's name; by saying we're sorry from the heart.

If it were really too late for any of us, it would have to mean that our distorted appearances, the poison, the eclipses and the prisons were all greater and more powerful than God's love. But we know that there is nothing on this earth or above greater than God and his love. Therefore, if we access God's love through Jesus and this "heart rending" all of those other things and the damage they have caused can be overcome. Not all at once, not very quickly either, but in nature, yes it is never too late.

## QUESTIONS

1. Have you come to believe that it is too late for you with God and with others?

   What does that mean?


2. Is there anything to these word, "Yet even now ..."?

   If you could believe it, how would it make a difference?


e. Even if it is "never too late," do you still doubt that it applies to you?

CHAPTER 14

GOD IS
# Welcoming

But he wanted it to be real, and he expressed
his doubts and desires out loud.
A prayer and a declaration.

"Faith given back to us after a night of doubt
is a stronger thing, and far more valuable to us
than faith that has never been tested."
—Elizabeth Goudge

Somewhere along the way, doubting got a bad rap. To be a doubter is to be a problem; to not be on board. Our faith is in question if we have questions. The patron saint of doubters of course is Thomas, one of Jesus's disciples. Nobody wants to be known as a "Doubting Thomas." Or do they?

I guess the first myth of the whole Thomas thing is the idea that doubt is the opposite of faith. I would say not. Doubt can be a pathway to faith. Churches and believers have often made a lot of people feel bad and just stay home because of doubts. It isn't written anywhere, but the assumption on Sunday morning in sanctuaries everywhere is that there isn't room for doubters. The tragedy of this is that everyone from the minister and priests to members are all sitting there with questions—doubts of all kinds.

If anything is the opposite of faith, it is fear. Whereas fear denies faith, doubt seeks clarification. Fear is that force that holds us back and down and keeps us from lifting off the ground by faith. Fear also keeps us from asking questions. I remember my ninth grade English teacher had a sign on the wall in the classroom which read, "The only stupid question is the one not asked." It's fear that keeps us from asking questions, let alone wanting answers.

Ah, but what is a good question? "Why" questions, for example, expect some kind of answer. This is not because there might be one; but because there was an expectation that comes from caring to know the truth.

Purely academic questions try to to poke holes in theories—these don't fit with doubt. There is a difference between a skeptic and a doubter. A skeptic has nothing invested in the answer; a doubter cares about the outcome. A skeptic asks the question from a distance; it is sport. But a doubter is different. A doubter is right there asking and invested in the outcome.

A doubter is a believer with questions. What is wrong with this? At some point, room for doubts and questions has begun to get smaller and smaller. Many pastors and priests seem to be avoiding the tough questions and answers. All the while, we have millions of people sitting in pews and chairs on Sundays wondering, "What is the point of being here?" and "How does this matter to my everyday life?" There are also millions more asking from Lowe's or IHOP or home, "Why should I go to church anymore with those hypocrites?" or "Why should I ever go back there?"

And yet the rope end is a real place, and it generates serious questions. Are we just supposed to leave questions like, "Have you forgotten me, Lord?" unanswered? Are we supposed to be silent when we are wondering if God can recognize us anymore? This is an essential question and one that is asked from a place of faith, not just desperation.

Enter Thomas. The first thing we have to remember about Thomas from earlier in the story is that he is a true believer; he says he is ready to die with Jesus (John 11:16). Like many of us, he started out with great faith when things were simpler. We remember faith when it was just the stories; it was easier. It gets harder when the questions come, when the doubts arrive.

The questions and doubts came for Thomas and the other disciples when Jesus was killed. It was that moment when everything they believed seemed to be erased. Wasn't he the Messiah? We have those moments too. Of course, for Thomas, it gets even more complicated when the risen Jesus appears to the disciples and not to him.

So Thomas does what any person who so wanted to believe that it was true would do. He says I want to see it, I want to touch it—then I'll believe (John 20:25). Isn't this is why we go to church—because we want to see it and touch it? Isn't this also why we don't go anymore—because we didn't find it there when we went? But the desire to believe doesn't go away that easily. Thomas could have let it go. He could have said nothing. But he wanted it to be real, and he expressed his doubts and desires out loud. Was it a prayer as well as a declaration?

Thomas is labeled as the doubter. Isn't this when Jesus is supposed to kick him out of the club? How dare he doubt!

But instead of shunning Thomas, Jesus invites him to see and touch and believe (John 20:27). Thomas, the "doubter," the guy who is allegedly raining on everybody's parade, is invited to come closer than anyone to the risen Christ.

Thomas' response to the invitation? "My Lord and My God!" says the one who so wanted it to be true and has it revealed to him in a most extraordinary way (John 20:28).

Wherever our doubts and questions come from—the living room, the shower, the fountain in the mall, the bar, the pew, or the park—and on whatever day, know where doubting leads. It leads us closer to God.

## QUESTIONS

1.  Which one are you—a skeptic or a doubter?

    Why and how do you know?

2.  Would you say that you were once a "true believer" like
    Thomas?

    Where did that faith go, or is it still there in some way?

3.  Could your turning doubts into prayers really lead you
    closer to God or at least to something unexpected about
    him?

# CHAPTER 15

## GOD IS

# Healing

### What do you want Jesus to do for you?

"Miracles are not contrary to nature,
but only contrary to what we know about nature."
—Augustine

Bart, like many at their end of the rope, was just sitting on the side of the road. Life and people had passed him by. He hadn't done anything especially wrong. He was broken and had a disability. It had been so many years. He had given up (Mark 10:46–52).

We get to this point ourselves. We come to expect … nothing more. *This is it*, we think. This is what we get. And if we are feeling extra masochistic on some days, we let ourselves dream of what we want or wanted. But that is stuff we keep buried; it is safer there. Life has this ability to melt or bend our expectations. There is some point, I can't tell you where for sure, when the expectations of our youth *become* different. It's not like they die. They just change or moderate. Sometimes it is slight, sometimes dramatic. But there is a point where we just … settle.

I think we expected more answers than questions. Instead we are left with so many more "Whys" than we ever thought possible. It is the lack of certainty about almost everything that is so hard. Things seemed to have more definition when we were younger. So many songs, books, and films—

the things that influence us or reflect life today are about "something to believe in" or finding something true. The questions still far outnumber the answers.

I think we expected desire to remain simple, but as we get older our desires and needs get complicated. We don't know the difference anymore. Either way, we just come to expect that we are never going to get what we really wanted or need (if we could know for sure); so we look for substitutes.

I think we also expected faith to follow some kind of pattern. Instead, our lives, church, other believers—intentionally or not—disrupt that pattern. When we were learning Bible stories as kids, it seemed understandable. Cry out for help, God hears it, and then he comes to the rescue—just like that, right? What happened to that formula? No more miracles; just bombshells, scares, and disruptions.

And so there is Bart on the side of the road. As far as we know, he's a simple guy. He doesn't expect much anymore. It is hard to tell much about him other than he was at the end of his rope.

And then one day, everything changed with a question asked of him.

It started with a "chance" encounter. Jesus of Nazareth happened to be walking by—something that didn't happen very often in those days. I think that is the first thing we can learn from Bart's story. There are no chance encounters with God.

From the end of his rope, from out of his blindness, Bart called to Jesus, acknowledging his divinity. People told Bart to be quiet and Jesus didn't respond to him. So he cried out louder. This time, Jesus "stood still" and told him to come closer. Think about this—Bart's cry made Jesus stand still. For those of us who are or who have cried out from the depths; this is a revelation.

So here he is standing in front of who he believes is God on earth. Imagine this! At the end of his rope, broken, forgotten, blind, and he gets to stand before Jesus. How does that feel? What could have been going through his mind? Well, if being invited into God's presence isn't enough, there is more.

Jesus asks Bart, "What do you want me to do for you?" The purpose of the question is almost as important as the person asking it. This is not a practical joke. This is not some kind of genie thing either. God walking the earth asking someone at the end of his rope what he wants. What could be more unexpected?

"What do you want me to do for you?" is a question that only in the stripped down, worn down time of the rope end can we hear clearly enough and are desperate enough to ask for what we really want—which of course seems impossible. As awful as the end of the rope is, one of the lessons is that it is awfully clarifying.

"What do you want?" my cousin and unofficial therapist Kristin asked once during a conversation about the future (she's good). I was thrown off. I could barely answer. I know what I want for lunch. But what do I want from God? What do I want from life? My sketchy answers at the time were as one could imagine—impossibilities.

Fortunately for Bart, he did not stumble or stammer. But he does ask for what seemed the impossible. "My teacher, let me see again," he tells Jesus (Mark 10:51). Not only does he ask for a miracle, but it just so happens that it is something that only God could help with. He doesn't ask for money or stuff or clarity. He doesn't ask for explanations and answers about the lost years of being blind or his being at the end of his rope. He asks God walking this earth to restore something about his life that he could not do or not even pretend to do himself.

At the end of the movie, *Field of Dreams*, Ray Cansella, who is at the end of his rope and about to lose his farm and livelihood says, "I've done everything I've been asked to do. I didn't understand it; but I've done it. And I haven't once asked what's in it for me." "What are you saying, Ray?" Shoeless Joe asks. "What's in it for me?" says Ray. Shoeless Joe responds, "Is that why you did this? I think you better stay here, Ray."

A lot of us feel like Ray Cansella when it comes to faith and life in general. We feel like we have done everything we have been asked to do. We often didn't understand it. And here we are at the end of our ropes wondering why and what happened. And the miracles—the miracles we read about in the Bible, never showed up for us.

Until this one day when Bart stands before Jesus and Jesus asks him what he wants.

The thing with God and miracles is this—they are a part of his character; as Bart's story shows, they are what he does, they are part of the plan—no coincidences. A miracle is defined as "an event that so overrides what observers understand of natural law that it creates wonder and serves as evidence of God's active intervention in the universe."[1] Long after we have given up and settled, the unexpected encounters with God, the impossible resolutions, the miracles and more are happening. Through him, "Whys?" become "Why nots?"

## QUESTIONS

1. Did you expect more answers from this life and from faith?

   Could you share some more about those expectations?


2. What do you want Jesus to do for you?

   Please say it out loud or write it down.


3. Are miracles still possible—miracles such as feeling the love of God after all of these years?

## CHAPTER 16

### GOD IS
# Loving

Once God has given his love to us,
he doesn't take it away.
That is because it is about him, not us.

"Jesus did not come to make God's love possible,
but to make God's love visible."
—Author Unknown

The word surreal seems to get used often these days. The world seems so off. We use the adjective *surreal* to capture the experience of things and events that seem out of the ordinary or beyond what we are used to—and what we are used to in this day and age is a lot. From terrorist attacks to personal drama, the limits of what we know as reality are getting pushed further and further. It is unsettling and uncomfortable. And even worse, most of what we call "real" is some kind of plastic version of what is real anyway. I mean, almost everything that we experience as real is mediated—it comes to us through some kind of channel—a facsimile or miniature version.

One thing that most of us might find surreal is God's way of loving. We have to come to have a distorted view of the way God designed love. Valentine's Day or dating shows on television—even our relationships—have warped love almost beyond recognition.

First of all, we think of love as something to go out and get. We have to find someone to love and someone to love us. We have to use various methods to "acquire" love. This happens in our family relationships as well as in church. We feel like we have to appear to be something we are not to gain the love of people. This is why we tell stories and make up stuff about ourselves. But this is an elaborate masquerade in which nothing real is gained or found—from beginning to end.

God's love is not something we have to achieve—it is already ours. We don't have to fool him or be something we are not with God. He already knows us better than we know ourselves. The Bible says he knit us together in our mother's wombs (Psalm 139:13–15). We know knitting is time consuming and an intricate activity that is done with great care. When somebody knits something it means they have put a lot of themselves into and they value it. That is what we mean to God. "God loves us not because of who we are, but because of who *he* is," goes the saying.

Another way we have distorted God's love is by making it about keeping or measuring it. We have turned love into a kind of game where how much money is spent and how many gifts are given is the measurement for love. I don't know whether to participate in or protest Valentine's Day anymore. It has some value, but at the same time it has become such an aberration of how God designed love. What is at the heart of measuring and earning love in our world? Fear. It is the fear of losing love and the fear of not being lovable. Think about it. Think about how much it drives us. Think about how restricting it all is. How many hours do we spend worrying if our spouses and others still love us?

The Bible tells us, "There is no fear in love, but perfect love casts out fear; for fear has to do with punishment … (1 John 4:18)." In other words, God's love is beyond earning and measure. No fear in love means not worrying about whether it will be lost. In fact, God's love is immeasurable in that it extends to the completely unlovable. Once God has given his love to us, he doesn't take it away. That is because it is about him, not us.

This is the other thing we have done with love—with God and with others—we have made it about ourselves. We seek out love for what it means to us. We look for friends and spouses who are going to do things for us. We only like God and church when they are doing something for us. "Where is "our" love?" we continuously ponder. Loving as we understand it is keeping our best to ourselves and demanding the best from others. We have made love about receiving when it was designed to be about giving. And then we wonder why it just doesn't work and why we don't feel loved.

God designed love to be about giving. And he demonstrated this. We have heard this verse in a million different ways; but hear it now in terms of love, "For God so loved the world that he gave his only son, so that everyone who believes in him may not perish but have eternal life (John 3:16)." God gives away his most precious part in loving us. Talk about surreal! God's love is about sacrifice, about loss.

God's love is freely ours; we don't have to keep earning it. When we take this in for the first time or yet again, it can be surreal and very real at the same time. It goes beyond our plastic and mediated existence. And yet we can scarcely imagine what it feels like. Maybe that's how we can begin to detect the difference between God's love and the world's love—this strange mix of real and surreal.

But in the end we need it to be real. The children's book, *The Velveteen Rabbit* offers a great illustration of real love, God's love:

"Real isn't how you are made," said the Skin Horse.

"It's a thing that happens to you. When a child loves

you for a long, long time, not just to play with, but REALLY loves you, then you become Real ... "[1]

I gave this book to my son Brian a few years ago. I inscribed it this way, "There is a saying in this book—'love makes you real.' Well, God's love made you real and your love has made me more real. Thank you. Merry Christmas. Love, Dada."

While God's love may feel surreal at first or forever, it is more real than anything we know. God's love keeps looking for us and when it finds us it yells out, "I found you!" It is the kind of love that keeps climbing the walls of anger around our souls; it opens our clenched fists. It is the kind of love that can break us free of the fears that pull on us.

Perhaps more than anything else in this world, we know God's love is real by its presence almost as much as by what feels like its absence. That is the essence of something being real.

## QUESTIONS

1. Which parts of your life seem the most surreal today?

2. How different is your definition of love from God's as described in this chapter?

   Which have you felt more—its absence or presence?

3. Can God's love be felt, really felt, such as through a comforting hand?

## CHAPTER 17

## GOD IS

# Comforting

### There we were all the time—in his love-wrought hands.

"It will greatly comfort you if you can see God's hand in both your losses and your crosses."

—C.H. Spurgeon

Have you ever wondered what God's hands are like? There was this older gentleman, Fred, in one of my churches. He was your typical, humble World War II vet that had always worked with his hands—outside, as a farmer and grounds manager. So whenever I shook his hand it felt like what I imagined God's hands to be like. Fred's hands were large, like a catcher's mitt. They were rough, dry, and worn. But when you shook his hand it had a gentle feel to it. His hand seemed to take your hand and enclose it. I imagine that must be how God's hands are.

It is hard to imagine God's hands when we are at the end of the rope. It is hard to feel God's hands when we feel so far away from God and anything representing God. Being at the end of our rope feels like we have basically slipped through the hands of God.

When we are crying out from the depths, it often feels like we are in free fall. Waiting to hit rock bottom—that place where we feel like we can't go any lower. And then sometimes we do go a little lower. But there definitely is a bottom. It is the place from which we cry out to God and others, the place where feel the most alone.

I remember when I hit the bottom. Everything had gone wrong. It was an awful time. I would just walk for hours with a cassette walkman and listen to depressing songs. I would take marathon naps. Then I would work at my part-time job and at night hide some more. I would lie awake and wonder where God was. I felt purposeless and empty. I went over it so many times in mind; I just couldn't figure out what was happening to me, why, and why then.

At some point, though, out of desperation, I thought of imagining resting in the palm of God's hand. At first, it seemed pathetic. I felt pathetic and broken. I had no where else to go. So I went with it. And night after night, I pictured myself in the palm of God's hand. And after a while it became comforting, very comforting. I think it began to work because I came to believe it—that there was a space for me in God's hand.

The amazing thing is that years later I would discover the following words in the Bible, "See, I have inscribed you on the palms of my hands … (Isaiah 49:16)." Imagine my surprise and wonder. Here I was, without knowing this verse, imagining a variation of this concept. At the end of my rope, the image of the palm of God's hand occurred to me. The times I have relied on that image to comfort me— both then and now—I might as well have been engraved or inscribed onto his hand.

I have shared this image and verse with a number of people now in my role as a pastor. I think especially of this time with a woman who was going through great difficulties. She had come to one of her bottoms. When I visited her at the hospital she was not well. I spoke with her and prayed with her. I asked God to hold her in the palm of his hand during this time. She thanked me and I left, saying I would come back soon. I returned about a week later. She could barely remember that I had visited before. But she started telling me how at some point during the week, she felt like she was being held in the palm of God's hand; that became her comfort. She added that she was wondering how she got that idea and that it had never occurred to her before. I smiled and told her it was a good idea and that she should continue to do this.

But it's not just God's hands that have the marks of love on them. Think of Jesus's hands. These are the hands through which nails were driven for love and for our salvation. Jesus invites Thomas to touch the mark in his hands (John 20:27). Jesus's hands still today bear the marks of the cross. Could it be a coincidence that the Old Testament talks about us being inscribed in the palm of his hand and in the Gospel Jesus's palms are where the nails pierced?

I know of so many people who probably did not know it, but who had felt God's hands upon them. There are brothers who were so low who were lifted up enough to go on. There are sisters who were at their ground zeroes and somehow felt sustained. It didn't take it away, but they got through and often that was a miracle in itself. Sometimes the only thing we can do is get through and just to do that we need a helping hand. This invisible hand reaches through the bars of our prisons and takes hold of our hand. It's the hand that reaches out and rests on our shoulders at the worst times of our lives.

By the way, our hitting bottom wasn't really the bottom at all. That awful place from which we have cried out so many times. It was us landing and sitting in the palm of God's hand. It is the same hand onto which he inscribed us. It is the same hand that was nailed to the cross for us. There we were all the time, in his love-wrought hands. There we were all the time, in the hands that never let us go.

## QUESTIONS

1. In what parts of your life do you need to be held in God's comforting hand, right now?

2. Try to picture the hand of God as well as the hands of Jesus.

   What do these hands mean to you?

3. Could the reach of these hands really be limitless?

   How far would they go to reach you?

## CHAPTER 18

GOD IS

# Treasuring

### It is about sparing no expense to find the one or ones who are lost— to risk it all, like at the cross.

"There is no one so far lost that Jesus cannot find him (or her) and cannot save him (or her)."
—Andrew Murray

It's very simple really: The math is easy to compute, and the logic is clear. In order to minimize losses and maximize gains, we keep and hold onto what we have and if we lose a few things along the way, it's okay because we are protecting the larger share of it, whatever *that* may be.

It could be things that are valuable to us. It could be money. It could even be family and friends. Hey, with each of those we are going to lose some during our lives, but as long as we are protecting the foundation, that is what matters. What matters is to protect our investments.

I think this is the thinking of a lot of churches. The "You're in my seat!" crowd is just protecting their church, right? "So what if a few people are turned away?" some think, "The core group is still here and the church is preserved." If a church loses a few members, that's okay; it's bound to happen, but as long as the main flock is there, everything is okay. All of this makes sense, right? It represents a kind of mindset that stands on the idea of whoever is already here matters most.

I mean, would it make much sense to spend a lot of money and use up people's time and energy looking for church members who have left or haven't been back in a while? If the resources are limited—which they usually are—then how can that be justified? They have to take care of the people who are still here. It doesn't seem wise to send the pastor or priest out to find these few people who have left when there are many more people already here that have needs.

And what about these people who have gone away or haven't shown up in a while? Isn't it their choice? If they want to stay home, that's what they are going to do. Or, of course, if they aren't following the Lord anymore that is their problem to deal with. Because if they got lost or separated from Jesus and our church, well, they must have done something that they shouldn't have. The Bible is pretty clear, so if they can't follow it and lose their way, what can be done for them? One bad apple could spoil the whole barrel, they say.

If they aren't looking for God, maybe they just aren't supposed to be in a church anyway. Again, the group is gathered here and it has many needs. Others will have to find their own way. Besides, evangelism, "the e-word" just makes everybody here feel uncomfortable; and why should the larger, gathered group be disrupted for just a few or even one?

Amen!?

Wait. Except one thing. There is a series of stories told by Jesus to people who thought along these lines that teaches the very opposite. For example, Jesus asks them if they would leave a flock of ninety-nine sheep to go off and find a lost one and not come back until they find it (Luke 15:1–7). In those days, leaving the flock would be pretty risky; wolves and other predators might find the sheep and then everything would be lost. All because of this one sheep who wandered away. But echoes of God's voice must have been ringing, "I will seek the lost, and I will bring back the strayed, and I will bind up the injured and I will strengthen the weak ... (Ezekiel 34:16)." Jesus adds that when he finds that lost sheep and brings it home, rather than scold it or separate it from the group to punish it, it is time to party.

And switching to theological terms, Jesus explains that it is the same for people and God. "Just so, I tell you, there will be more joy in heaven over one sinner who repents than over ninety-nine righteous persons who need no repentance (Luke 15:7)."

What kind of thinking is this? What kind of show is God running up there? How can you have more joy over the one sinner than the ninety-nine righteous people? I am no numbers guy for sure, unless I am missing something, but this math is off.

Jesus doesn't stop there. He then tells some more crazy stories. He shares a story about a woman who loses one out of ten coins and turns the house upside down to find it (Luke 15:8–10). And like before, when she does, she wants to party too. He sweetens the deal by saying, "Just so, I tell you, there is joy in the presence of the angels of God over one sinner who repents (Luke 15–10)."

The last story Jesus tells is the one about the son who takes his share of the money, wastes it on immoral pursuits (Luke 15:11–32). Notice how he switches from sheep to coins to people. Anyway, the son finds himself at his lowest, his own rope end, and decides to change his ways and come back to his father. He is lovingly received by his father but resented by his brother who "stayed" faithful to their father all those years.

Shouldn't there be some consequences for the wasted money and immoral living? Certainly from the perspective of the brother. Instead the father says, "But we had to celebrate and rejoice, because this brother of yours was dead and has come to life; he was lost and has been found (Luke 15:32)."

Aha! See, this is what good news is about. Therefore, it is what God is about. It is about sparing no expense to find the one or ones who are lost—to risk it all, like at the cross, to seek out those who have lost their way, and to not come back until they are found. When they do come home, we must welcome them with a party, no matter how long they were gone, no matter how far they ventured, and no matter what mistakes occurred. No questions asked. No ifs, ands, or buts. No lectures or advice.

I know, I know, it doesn't compute. It goes against all logic. Even the logic of Star Trek's Mr. Spock, who said, "The needs of the many outweigh the needs of the one or the few."[1] It goes against a lot of tradition and thinking. But this is God's character. Who is God's heart set on and breaking for? God is seeking the one who has been forgotten, lost, hidden, broken, and trapped. Because for God, the gains are not in terms of protecting big numbers and widely-held assets, but in the redemption of the forgotten.

## Questions

1. Do you see the logic and math of maintaining the group instead of going after the one?

   What remaining doubts do you have?


2. What if this is God's character?

   What if Jesus's stories are true representations?

   Could God be searching for you right now?

   What does it mean to you?


3. And if you are "found," isn't possible that there might be a place on earth where the homecoming party can happen?

CHAPTER 19

GOD IS

# Providing

Churches are the places through which God has
chosen to begin to put the broken pieces
of our lives as well as
the pieces of his kingdom together.

"Christian brotherhood is not an ideal which we must
realize; it is rather a reality created by God in Christ in
which we may participate."[1]

—Dietrich Bonhoeffer

Imagine a Sunday morning in which the bread and cup
are being shared and passed around the pews among the
living and the dead; black and white; executed murderer
and victim; the blind, widows, and children. And while they
are who they are, at the same time they are also healed
and whole and in community together. Time and divisions
and death are conquered as all of these people are seated
together in a church during the sacrament of the Lord's
Supper sharing in complete reconciliation, all the while the
congregation is singing "Blessed Assurance." It is a perfect
picture of communion. Sounds a little bit like heaven but
it is actually the closing scene from the 1984 film, *Places in
the Heart.*

Though a film, it offers a beautiful vision of what God intended for Sunday morning, really every morning among his children.

In fact, the Bible shows us the first and greatest example of what a Christian community or a congregation is supposed to be. "Now the whole group of those who believed were of one heart and soul, and no one claimed private ownership of any possessions, but everything they owned was held in common. With great power the apostles gave their testimony to the resurrection of the Lord Jesus, and great grace was upon them all. There was not a needy person among them ... (Acts 4:32–34)"

You see, according to this, no one is saying, "You're in my seat!" Nobody is divided by long-term members and visitors. No one is seated according to their degree of holiness or sinfulness.

Quite the opposite. This biblical or Holy Spirit-shaped version of Christian community basically emphasizes four things. The first is unity, "one heart and soul." The second is that everything was shared. The third is that they kept their eyes on the resurrected Jesus, and this worship blessed everyone. The fourth, which was the fruit of the first three, was that *all* the needs of people were met. And as a whole, as a system, everyone was valued no more and no less than anyone else—all as children of God and believers.

Author and professor John Patton writes, "God is the author of community, creating it as an expression of human relationality ... It is brought into being through human action, empowered through relationship to God."[2] Think about that—God as the author of community, writing his story through our lives.

But just look around. Churches and society are experiencing an unprecedented breakdown of community and shared life. There is plenty of blame to go around—first our own choices and actions, but also television and the

Internet creating distance between people. There are also world and neighborhood divisions and conflicts that build walls. There is also alienation—a result of negligence.

Part of why the state of churches today is so heartbreaking is because it is so far off the vision. And it is particularly distressing because in most cases, the fault line for the devastation is along relationships—with God and with brothers and sisters. The church, in the end, is God's instrument for saving living, real-time relationships through Jesus. If relationships are about communication, shared times, lives and stories; and for growing and building up— then the church serves as *the* place where we connect with God and with other believers.

A few years ago, Chase Bank had a marketing line that went, "The right relationship is everything." While they were speaking about banking, churches and believers must say and live the same thing. This connection to God and to brothers and sisters in Christ is sacred. Not only is it sacred in nature, but it was also meant to be lived as sacred—in other words, intensely valued and cherished. The theological word for an intensely valued or cherished relationship is covenant. We are in covenant with God and with each other through Jesus's death on the cross. But it didn't just end there: A covenant is a living, breathing thing consisting of love, sacrifice, remembrance, and care.

Patton also explains, "God continues in relationship with creation by hearing us, remembering us, and bringing us into relationship with one another. Human care and community are possible because of being held in God's memory; therefore, as members of caring communities we express our caring analogically with the caring of God by also hearing and remembering."[3] Meaning that churches are not just buildings of people with activities but the scene of God's grace and care as expressed through the lives and times of God's people. Whether they are 50 or 10,000 members, God is doing much more at a church than we could ever realize.

That is why when people tell me that they can be believers and not go to church, I am skeptical. I understand why they want to stay home, believe me I do. But with God as the "author" of community, and the church as the instrument of connection, to be without those is to be incomplete. And further, that churches fall short of God's intention is not a valid excuse for staying home either—that makes it more about the people than about God—given what we are talking about here—that is just not true.

Churches are the places through which God has chosen to begin to put the broken pieces of our lives as well as the pieces of his kingdom together. It is slow and often painful and doesn't look like it's working a lot of the time. But quietly, patiently, and purposefully he re-"members" his children through his hands and ours.

There may be nothing like a Sunday morning in America. But as God conceived and created it, there truly is nothing like a community of believers—of one heart and soul, resurrection-focused, and meeting all the needs of one another—the joys, the concerns and the pains. And not just on Sunday morning, but every morning, everyday. Yes, it is meant to be as close as it comes to heaven on earth—a foretaste of the kingdom to come.

## QUESTIONS

1.  What are some reasons why you find this description of
    a church as a "heaven on earth" to be unbelievable?

    Can you share some church-related experiences that
    felt more like "hell on earth?"

2.  What do you think about God being the "author of
    community," and what does it mean for where you
    might be in your faith today?

3.  How can Jesus stand between us and other believers
    and their judgments if we aren't there?

CHAPTER 20

## GOD IS

# Saving

So not only does he stand between her and the stones, he pours out his grace upon her and gives her a do-over.

"I deserve to be damned, I deserve to be in hell;
but God interfered!"
—last words of John Allen
of the Salvation Army

Their arms were raised, rocks in hand. Their rage was boiling over. They were aiming for her head—that would get her right away. But they had to wait for the teacher's answer.

What was taking so long? What is he writing in the sand there anyway? After all, we caught her in the very act of adultery. And the law is clear about this...

We know this story of the woman caught in adultery (John 7:53, 8:11). Fortunately, for her and for all of us, the stones were dropped that day.

She was at the end of her rope. As much as it has been romanticized in films and television, adultery is damaging for all involved. So here she was committing adultery, a sin, but on top of it, the officials catch her and are ready to impose the sentence. By the way, what were they doing there—adultery patrol?

But seriously, as a bonus, they figure they can use this as a way to get Jesus in trouble at the same time. They present the case and the guilty party to him and ask what he thinks, hoping to trap him. And that is when he starts writing in the ground.

I know this doesn't happen today exactly as it is described, but the players seem similar. Churches today sometimes have their share of people (pastors and church-goers) who are on "sin patrol," watching for especially sinful sinners. And when they aren't on patrol, they are busy creating an atmosphere in which sinners feel the heat and don't feel comfortable. They do this of course by trading their stones for frowns as well as outright judgmental comments, which feel like stones.

And somehow the sinners of today find the pain of the frowns and rejection not much worse than the stones. At least with the stones, a person died. Today, a sinner gets "frowned" and leaves the church; there is that pain, but also the sting of seeing the frowners at the mall or grocery store.

But the message that Jesus shares is clear: We are *all* sinners. "Let anyone among you who is without sin be the first to throw a stone at her (John 8:7)." The story tells us that one by one they left until they were all gone, leaving Jesus and the woman.

He stood there for her between the judgment and sentence. It is a beautiful portrait. But that is not all he did for her.

"Woman, where are they? Has no one condemned you?" She said, "No one, sir." And Jesus said, "Neither do I condemn you. Go your way and from now on do not sin again (John 8:10–11)."

And can we see that she was nobody special. She didn't have to do anything for Jesus to earn his grace. She didn't have to attend any classes. She doesn't even make some kind of profession of faith in him. And yet, there just isn't any doubt that she went on her way with her heart belonging to Jesus. He does all the work.

So not only does he stand between her and the stones, he pours out his grace upon her and gives her a do-over. And by doing this, something else happens. With Jesus in the midst or in the middle, we are all equal. All the emphasis we put on whether we are good enough or holy enough dissolves in his true presence. All the games we play and the words we use to assess, quantify, and evaluate our faith or our values or those of other people don't compute with Jesus. All the time that is spent today calculating who is a real Christian and who isn't, is met with quiet writing in the sand by Jesus. With him there aren't the sinners and the holy ones. He doesn't even condemn the stoners. Nobody is any less or more guilty in Jesus's eyes. See, there is a difference between condemnation and conviction. Condemnation says, "Because of these things you are doing, you're going to hell"; conviction says, "These things you are doing just show that you need Jesus to jump in."

I love how the film, *The Passion of the Christ* portrayed this scene in a flashback. The character of the woman is on the ground at Jesus's feet and she is grasping for his ankles. And then from the top of the screen, his hand slowly descends and takes her hand and begins to lift her up. That is exactly what he does for her and, in many ways, for us today.

Know what? Everybody wants (and needs) a second chance. We have all made mistakes. We have all sinned. And we have a bunch of things we have done in life that we regret; they aren't going away. And God in his holiness and righteousness could throw the book at us. Hands down, we would lose our case—guilty every time. But instead of condemning us all, he sets up the ultimate do-over. This is our second chance in Jesus, and there is no depth so great that he can't reach us and lift us up. When we are at the end of our rope and the frowns are being aimed at us, he is still there.

The truth is that we all are caught in the very act. This is the nature of sin and us; we may not have the sin patrol on us, but God knows we deserve the consequences for our sins. And many of us don't even need the frowns cast our way. We do enough damage to ourselves by holding the poison of guilt within us for years.

The difference for us today is that when the frowns are cast, because of Jesus's work on the cross and our faith in him, the frowns can fall away. And, through that same faith, we are lifted up, acquitted of all our charges, to restart.

## QUESTIONS

1. What did it feel like when frowns have been thrown your way?

2. How does it feel to know that Jesus's grace is stronger and matters more than any human judgments?

3. Although it can't be seen, how does it feel to know the judgments are temporary and the grace is eternal?

## CHAPTER 21

# GOD IS

# Eternal

## The unseen are the things that are sacred and will last forever.

Remember those books that we had as kids that revealed messages with a special marker? They seemed to be a lot fun at the time. It was the surprise of the message appearing and wondering how it worked. But, somewhere along the way we lost our comfort with mystery and the unseen. As adults we can barely stand surprises let alone what God might be working on that we can't see. All we want now are "behind the scenes" looks and documentaries explaining everything. At work, the department just wants to see results. At home, our spouses just want to see how much we love them. Seeing, as you know, is believing.

But is that really true? Because it seems like the more we see, the more we distrust and question. We don't seem any better off for the increased visibility. Think about it, nearly everything has become visible. Have you noticed how there are televisions everywhere? From the handheld ones to the car ones to the ones in grocery stores; they are everywhere!

This feeds the idea that only the visible is real. I mean, as humans we would have struggled with the unseen anyway, but with nearly everything on screens now, we are in even bigger trouble. It all feeds the idea that only the visible matters.

The problem is that most of what is visible or seen isn't sacred. And yet, I know we are all crying out for the sacred; we grieve its gradual disappearance, and we would do something more about it but we can't take our eyes off the screens. We have been hypnotized by the vile, the exploitive, the explicit, and the profane—all because we need some entertainment and some distraction, they say.

But it's not just the screens we need to see to make us real, it's the stuff too. Think of all those self-storage places and attics filling up with things. If I (and others) can't see my wealth, my possessions, my visible worth, well then I have no value.

Late at night the infomercials start their serenade of sweet riches as we doze off and the television light flickers in the dark. From real estate to telemarketing, we can make thousands of dollars a month. We can leave that dead end job soon after starting this or that program. The networks talk to us like we're old friends. It is all a grotesque overture of how addicted we have become to all things visible—and how the sacred or eternal is disappearing from view.

It's like this with addictions as well. With no drink or bottle in sight, we panic. Without access to the internet, we wonder how we can access our favorite porn site on another PC. A day away from our desk at work for many of us is empty and makes us jittery. These things that eclipse the light in our lives basically become our companions. And to not have them in sight is terrifying. The madness of all of this is that none of it is permanent. So many of us are attached to things that will expire, run out, or die. None of it is going to last.

From the satellite view to the cameras on the scene all the way down to the room in which we sit, we can see all of it and yet none of this sight gives us vision—vision to see what really has value. If it makes any sense, we are blinded by what we see. We are fixated on the temporary because it is all we can see. In many ways, the temporary is easier. It's there. And yes we know it won't be there forever, but it's here now; and we are a "now" people—"right now" people.

Perhaps one of the reasons why God seems less and less present in the world and in our lives is because we see the eternal less and less. It's not just a matter of sight; we're not even seeking it much anymore. We hear that many people are seeking the spiritual, and that is a good thing. But even that has taken on a "seen" or "showy" character.

Listen to these words from the Bible, "Even though our outer nature is wasting away, our inner nature is being renewed day by day. For this slight momentary affliction is preparing us for an eternal weight of glory beyond all measure, because we look not at what can be seen; for what can be seen is temporary, but what cannot be seen is eternal (2 Corinthians 4:16–18)."

It may be a long time, but we know this: We've glimpsed, if not taken in, "what cannot be seen." For example, seen is the kiss and affection and unseen is the connection between two hearts. Or, seen is the pretense and illusion of having it all together and unseen is a soul truly at peace. Seen is needing the affirmation of others to feel worthy; unseen is knowing that God accepts us completely through Jesus. Seen is the accumulation of money and things; unseen is the wealth of a heart and soul connected to God. Seen are the dreams and desires based on society's demands and expectations; unseen is the quiet confidence that God has already designed our futures beyond our imagination. In each case, the seen are things that will not last no matter how hard we try to hold on. But the unseen, these are the things that are sacred and will last forever.

I don't know why God has made the most important things invisible. It would have been a lot easier if we could see God and these eternal rewards. If faith were a little like those books with the hidden messages and we had the marker that revealed messages from God—now that would be cool. But in some ways the Bible is like that. And maybe God set it up like this—with seen and unseen things—so that we might have a chance to recognize the difference between the sacred and the material, between the eternal and the temporary.

I wonder if our vision of God and the eternal things could be improved by closing our eyes more. At least when our eyes are closed they are no longer fixed on screens and stuff for a few moments. Yes, I know it's dark, mysterious, and we can't see. And yet, we can begin to see much more than with our eyes open.

## QUESTIONS

1.  It feels like nothing is sacred anymore.

    What happened?

    How do you see this in your experience?

2.  How many things with which you are involved that won't die, expire, run out, or end can you name?

3.  If we do close our eyes to this world more to improve our vision, will we be able to see or hear God more clearly? Please say some more about that.

## Chapter 22

## God Is
# Speaking

### The sound of her name spoken by Jesus reaches her at the end of her rope.

"Caring is remembering. Remembering is caring.
This is affirmed in both the Old and New Testaments by
the picture of God's remembering God's people ..."[1]
—John Patton

The most familiar and soothing sound to our ears is, of course, our name. Research has shown that we respond more to it physiologically and emotionally than any other sound. It could be because we have heard it more than any other word or sound. Or it could be that we associate so much with this one word. This is why politicians, for example, use the interviewer's name over and over and it sounds so phony to us listening. "Jim, that is a great question; I really appreciate you asking that, Jim. Let me tell you, Jim, my answer is ... ."

The use of our names conjures up many memories. We fondly recall the echo of our names in the neighborhood at dinner time. As well, the whisper of goodnight and our names is still especially comforting. Of course our names being used as a joke or screamed in anger over and over isn't so fondly remembered.

Naming or names are so important that, as we remember, it is one of the first things Adam does—"and whatever the man (Adam) called every living creature, that was its name" (Genesis 2:19).

It's often not so much how our name is used as much as the fact that it is used or *remembered*. We all know how awful it feels when people can't remember our names. The "Hello, My Name Is" name tag glance doesn't make us feel any better either. When people use our names, it means we are valued. It means that we matter. The voiced name or the one on the list means something.

I don't know which comes first—our names are forgotten more and more or that we no longer listen or expect to hear our names. Either way, many of us start to reach a point or begin to exist in a state where we can't hear our name anymore. Actually, we don't need a hearing check. It is a soul thing. When we feel forgotten or distanced from God and others we just don't listen for our names anymore.

Other stuff happens, too, that affects our senses. Grief diminishes our vision and hearing. Almost everything slows down when we are grieving and crying out. And besides, when we are crying out, we can barely hear anything else. When we find ourselves in a prison the sound is no good— just echoes. As we know, when we are in a prison it is very difficult to connect with God or others. It's just the way it is. Anger and disappointment also dull our hearing. Anger acts as a wall around our soul—and it's sound proof.

As much as our senses might be affected, we never stop longing to hear our name—that most familiar sound. As far away as we go, as long as it has been and as disconnected as we might become, our ears and souls still long to hear it. Think about this, we still long to hear our name spoken by ones whose voices we can no longer hear. We often wonder what our name would sound like now on the phone or in person from lost loved ones or even friends from long ago.

It was probably like this for Mary Magdalene after Jesus died. Days earlier, she watched the man she loved and believed was God walking this earth, die. He was gone. She was there; she watched it at the foot of the cross. She was devastated and overwhelmed with grief and disappointment (John 20:1–16).

And just like we often do, she went to the grave early Sunday morning. Having made many visits to the grave myself, I know the feeling. We sit or stand there with the tears, questions, loneliness, and quiet. It's so quiet. And we secretly hope for a chance meeting. I know I used to hope that maybe I would see my mother—just a glimpse; just to know.

Like I said, at the end of the rope, things are kind of fuzzy. So when Mary Magdalene was standing outside Jesus's tomb—which they thought had been broken into, his body stolen—strange things start happening. She looked inside and saw two angels who spoke to her. After her brief conversation with them, she turned around to see a man.

"Woman why are you weeping? Whom are you looking for?" he asked (John 20:15). The story goes that she thinks he is the gardener. But this is what the rope end does to us—we can be staring right at God and still not see. Mary, at the end of her rope, with Jesus alive and right in front of her, can't see him. Instead, she wonders where the body has been taken. We do this—when God is speaking directly to us we look for what we thought he was to us and our lives. Or another way of looking at it is to say that we often operate as if Jesus was still dead or didn't rise.

So what was Jesus to do? She was blinded by her grief and disillusionment; there was no reaching her, as would we say. Here he was standing before her, alive again, and speaking to her. What could he do to reach her at the end of her rope?

"Jesus said to her, 'Mary!'" (John 20:16). Her name. He doesn't say woman or friend. He doesn't say, "Hey, it's me Jesus." He doesn't shake her nor does he give up and walk away. He says that most familiar sound, "Mary." And it is what breaks through. It is the sound that reaches her at the end of the rope.

Could it be that simple? Remember that our names are more than a sound or word. Our names, when said in love as God does, mean we matter, it means we are remembered and valued. Remembering that people don't need lectures and advice like, "get over it," but maybe after the funeral just need to hear their names at the front door or on the phone. But it is not just widows and widowers who need to hear from us—all who are at the end of their ropes need it. The cool thing is God has also been saying our names through others in our times of despair. The phone call, the visit, the card or encouraging conversation—they were all examples of how the Lord speaks our names.

More than any other voice, more than compliments and sweet whispers, the words we long to hear are our names spoken by God as he treasures and loves us more than we can ever know. Our names are given to us at birth, and their meaning changes over time. Other people may have the same name, but it becomes uniquely ours in our lives. Yet, the value of our names and our lives never changes in God's mind. God not only remembers our names, but God speaks our names even now, through our grief and doubt and our darkness. He calls out our names directly or through the voices of others, even when we can't or won't hear him.

## QUESTIONS

1. If you could hear God saying your name through all the noise and things, how would it sound?

   Please try to imagine the sound of it.


2. How would you rate your spiritual hearing, on a scale from clear to deaf?

   What can be done to improve spiritual hearing?


3. Can our hearing and other parts of our lives somehow be made new?

CHAPTER 23

GOD IS
# Restoring

## God takes old, beat up, worn down things and makes them new.

> "The house of my soul is too small for you to come to it.
> May it be enlarged by you. It is in ruins, restore it."
> —Augustine Prayer

Everybody loves new things, right? We want new houses and new cars and other new stuff. One of the main ways things are marketed to us is by simply calling it new. It may have been on the shelf for decades, but just print new on it and voila!

Because the truth is, in the end, we aren't so cool with new when it comes to real stuff. Real stuff like faith, church, relationships, or life in general.

It is a fear thing: New is dangerous, unpredictable. When we approach something new, that force starts pulling on us; after a while, we kind of back off, claiming it wasn't the right time or the best way to go.

But that is only part of why we avoid the new. It is also because we love holding onto the old. As destructive and damaging as the old might be, we hold onto it—we clutch and cling to it. The old (or the present) is a known quantity, and it's comfortable. We have to maintain that equilibrium.

We hold onto relationships even though they are destructive because at least we know it is destructive. Something or someone new might be worse or it might be better—but it is the not knowing that is so hard to face.

There is something else about the new. There is the thinking that we don't deserve anything new. At the rope end, we think we are beyond help, beyond deserving. When we are at the end of the rope for so long, we kind of accept that nothing new will be coming our way.

When the poison of guilt and sin is eating us away down to our bones, it is difficult, impossible even, to imagine that any kind of new thing can be done. Really.

So even worse, we start to believe that something new isn't even possible at the end of our rope. This is a vision thing. We close our eyes to everything because it is truly unbearable to watch anymore. But at the same time we are turning away from the horror of it all, we might also be missing something else going on. Even if something new was happening, we might miss it anyway because we have given up on looking for it, or have become blind to it.

Whether it is that we don't recognize it, or believe it isn't even possible anymore, or we fear it, or feel like we don't deserve it, we reject the new time and time again in favor of holding onto our old ways and things.

"Do not remember the former things, or consider the things of old. I am about to do a new thing; now it springs forth, do you not perceive it?" (Isaiah 43:18–19) In this Old Testament verse we get another clue about God's character. In this as well as other places, God speaks of being all about the new.

But we need to be clear about what kind of new. God's new is about restoration; not replacement. See, I think we confuse replacement with restoration. God doesn't work that away. He takes the broken pieces and puts them back together—better than before. God takes old, beat-up, worn down things and makes them new. And often, while he is trying to do this, we are at the front desk asking for a replacement—for which there isn't one. So while we are complaining about the service and why there isn't a replacement, God is wrestling with us to attach broken pieces in a stronger and more blessed arrangement.

Many believers and churches struggle with God making things new. What looks like chaos is often rejected. What looks like change often causes division and confusion. And yet, could it be that God was doing a new thing?

God does "new" things whether we see them or not. In other words, just because our world or our lives do not look new, it doesn't mean God isn't working.

In fact, God says, " ... See I am making all things new" (Revelations 21:5). To which we say, all things? Because we look at the world and see that most things appear to be getting worse. So how can God say, "I am making all things new?" This is a vision of the future.

We could look at the world and our lives and say they are all falling apart. It feels like that often. Yet, it reminds me of when something is being restored or made new. For example, when a piece of furniture is being restored, it has to be worn down and the surface has to be stripped and removed before the new finish can be applied.

So, could God be making the world and our lives both so radically new that we can't see it or don't want to see it? Maybe the restoration prep steps for us require a lot of stripping and scratching. In order to make us new, God has to cut through our fears, our doubts, our sense of worthlessness, and our blindness. That is a lot of layers to wear down before anything new can come.

God doesn't just put a "new" sticker on us and try to pass us off as something we're not. It wouldn't be God's way to repackage us and claim we are new. His restoration and making things new isn't about the surface and the presentation—it's about restoring our hearts and souls (Psalm 51:10; Psalm 23:3).

# QUESTIONS

1.  Why do we fear new things or newness?

    What is it about the new that scares us? Please share from your perspective.


2.  Is there any chance God could be doing a new thing in your life that is not easily seen?


3.  If there is even the smallest chance that God is doing something new purposefully, then could it also mean that there might be a bigger plan for the world and for your life?

CHAPTER 24

GOD IS

# Purposeful

There is no chance, there is no fate, there are no
coincidences with God; he loves us too much
for anything about us to be random.

"I have lived a long time and the longer I live
the more convincing proofs I see
that God governs in the affairs of men."
—Benjamin Franklin

It is easy to look at this world and say that God is not in
control. Wars, violence, hatred, brokenness—our world
seems filled with everything that isn't God. We could think,
"Maybe God was involved in the world before, but it seems
like he has left the building."

There just doesn't seem like there is any order or purpose
to what is happening. Many of us were taught and grew up
believing in a "big" God. We trusted in a God that held the
world and our lives in his hands. We remember the hymn-
turned-pop song, "He's got the whole world in his hands."
What happened?

But it is not just the world. So many things happen to us
in our own lives everyday that make us wonder about God's
presence, let alone his providence. It is very hard to see
and detect a pattern to the events of our lives. It's all over
the map. It just seems so indiscriminate. A win here, a loss

there; mostly split decisions, though. Random has a kind of worthlessness to it; whereas purpose indicates care. That's what we are missing in all this.

We have talked a lot about being at the end of the rope, with "Why?" as the signature question. So, why would God let us get to the end of our rope? Why would God let a rope end exist in the first place?

Now, what about this idea of purpose? I know we say there's a purpose for all things as a way of rationalizing terrible things. We call it fate or chance or coincidence and leave it at that.

But is it fate that many of us have been told by others at church that we were in their seats or space or ministry and told to leave? I mean, if everything is fated, then I guess the mistreatment of a lot of people by believers and churches was designed. Cruel, to say the least.

Is it chance that a lot of men just happen to click on and view some porn on the Internet and a few weeks later can't stop? Or is it chance that something harmless like a job or one drink crosses our path and not long after it totally eclipses everything that really matters in our lives? These are true yet astonishing random occurrences—if that's what they are.

Is it coincidence that at the lowest times of our lives— when we are crying out from the depths—we feel the most alone? Isn't that when we need people the most? Everybody's there for the funeral, but a few days later nobody is calling anymore. When we have been there or are there now, there is not a soul around and God seems to be gone too. This is quite an awful coincidence.

Unless ... "We know that all things work together for good for those who love God, who are called according to his purpose" (Romans 8:28).

This raises three main questions. First, does this mean that God is working through "all things" for a good purpose?

Second, what is that purpose? Third, why isn't this work always visible?

Well, yes, God is working through all things together for our good. It starts with the fact that God is omniscient, present, and potent: God knows all things, is everywhere (Holy Spirit) and has the power to do all things. So we start with the idea that is it possible for God to make all things work together for good.

Then there is the point of "all things." Does it mean that all the catastrophes and calamities and seasons or lifetimes at the end of the rope are part of some plan for good? Yes.

Which brings us to the purpose or plan behind it all. What is this good? The good is of course our welfare and provision (Jeremiah 29:11). But more to the point; the good God is going to make happen is our hearts belonging to him. That is where all of this is going. That is where all of this has always been heading, for the whole world.

And that leads us to visibility. Why can't we always see this "good" that God is working through all things in our existence? One reason could be that we are not fully convinced that "all things" are being worked for the good. How can we see what we don't believe?

And yet, we have to keep in mind that this is the way God has always been working. According to the Bible, he created and organized the world out of a shapeless void. As well, he sends Jesus into the brokenness and chaos of the human existence to save it. God consistently chooses to accomplish his purposes through human lives and history—whether it has been called providence or not.

But there is another part to the visibility. If God is working for our good, then shouldn't "all things" be good? I mean why should there be any bad in this path to good. That is where our vision comes in. It often seems to be blocked or diminished. By what? Our sins, our pride, the way we want things—just to name a few.

Here is God's challenge with us. We are stubborn, slow learning, proud, not very good listeners, and easily distracted. He is good and somehow has to find a way through all of our messes and mistakes, heartbreaks and confusion to turn our hearts fully towards him. For many of us, it might take years, even lifetimes. There are some great stories about people becoming saved on their deathbeds. In other words, the sum total of their lives builds up to just one faithful moment. The challenge for God is self-imposed. He loves us and values us so much as his creation that instead of programming us like robots, he works through this broken world and the broken pieces of our lives to reach our hearts.

Yes, he is in control. Which brings us to the million dollar question: So God's plan was for us to be alienated from church and get addicted to porn and feel so lonely and isolated as well as so many other awful things ... for our good?

Let me ask you this: Would we be reading this book if we or someone we loved weren't at the end of the rope? Could God, who is moving us toward the good, allow or permit rope ends to come into our lives, all the while holding us in his hand, so that we might reach a point of asking for a do-over?

There is no chance, there is no fate, there are no coincidences with God; he loves us too much for anything about us to be random. Our births, our families, our lives, our mountaintops and triumphs; our rope ends and dead ends; our insights and mysteries are all pointing towards and moving towards one thing: our hearts belonging to God. No matter what it looks like, no matter how bad it gets, it is still in God's hands and moving toward good.

As many times as we have asked God in prayer, "Why?" he has answered, "Because I love you and I want your heart to belong to me."

## QUESTIONS

1. What would it mean if you believed and lived as if God was in control and had plans for you beyond your circumstances and vision?

2. How often do you think of something as a coincidence and now may be wondering if it was something more? Please think of some specific examples.

3. Can all the bad and disappointments and questions still all be moving toward "good" in God's hands?

# Part Three

## A SECOND CHANCE OFFERS ... POSSIBILITY

"Christ has transformed all our sunsets into dawn."
—Clement

It is in the light of each marvelous and glorious sunrise that we can see ... possibility. What the darkness hides and blurs and distorts; the light illuminates and clarifies and restores.

It is the same way for the view from the rope end. In the "light" and memory of the box of Polaroids of God's heart, we can see possibilities again—potential outcomes that until now seemed impossible. Up until now we just caught glimpses of them. But I know that can't be enough. We've come too far to just leave it at the pictures. What about experiencing what the pictures showed?

More and more DVD's are coming out with something called "alternate endings" where different options for conclusion of the movie or show were filmed but not used. The director usually offers the reasons for the choice in the commentary feature. But the cool thing is that we get to see what might have happened.

Could there be alternate endings to our lives? In other words, a continuation or conclusion on the other side of this rope end that might be more desirable than what we envision right now. Because the way it looks for so many of us, this might be one of those stories where the main character has a tragic end.

Could there be an ending that the "director" has already completed, waiting for us? How about the one in which the anger finally disappears? Is there an outcome through which we come out from behind our masks? Could there be a conclusion in which the effect of the poison in our systems is reversed? Can a finale exist during which we find real, true joy in this life? Is there an ending where we experience healing? Has a finish been written in which we experience the presence, comfort, and power of God in our daily lives? Is there an ending in which we feel forgiven and able to forgive others?

These certainly exist. And it is inspiring just to think about them. But the thing with endings is the "how." How can we access these kinds of living or soul alternate endings? Clearly, it is not as easy as using the remote. There is a way, though. I will share that with you later, but for now let's just explore the possibilities. Let's see what life and faith could be like.

It is in the promising and emergent light of a sunrise that we see the landscape differently. The same things we see each and every day can somehow look different with a sunrise. Maybe it is the lighting. Or maybe it is just the idea that something new has begun—a new day. And each time we are given the gift of a new day, we have the gift of another chance.

# CHAPTER 25

## A SECOND CHANCE OFFERS
# Truth

## What looks horrible and awful in the dark becomes comprehensible and hopeful in God's light and love.

> "The truth will make you free,
> but first it will make you miserable."
> —Tom DeMarco
> author and teacher

Remember how we talked about being "as sick as our secrets"? What happened was awful. But what makes it even worse, even more damaging, is that it is not the truth yet. It is hidden, and that is where it does the most damage. It keeps shaping us in destructive ways. Much like a fungus that grows in the dark, it grows and takes over after a while.

There is also this strange light of God-blocking eclipse that colors everything. And while God's light still shines around it, the obstruction colors everything we do. Just to deal with it we say, "There is nothing wrong; there's no problem." Denial keeps us from the truth—it can be stories, lies, or rationalizations. We try to convince ourselves that everything is okay when it is not.

One of our worst fears is that we have become unrecognizable to ourselves, to others and to God. Our real face replaced by a mask. But even with the masks, which are usually for protection, we grieve not being who we thought we were or were supposed to be. But it seems so far away, and the only thing to do is to embrace the mask.

The resolution for this story is pretty textbook. We know how it is going to go. We are going to stay hidden so no one can find the real us. We are the life of the party so that no one looks any further. Maybe they will and maybe they won't. But the longer we hide, the more we disappear. The more that we fade away, the more we wear the mask. In addition to that, we are going to exist in this strange light of denial, never experiencing real joy or real pain. And that is okay, we think, that is the way we want it. But at the end of this kind of story, at the end of our lives, people won't know what to say about us; they will have never known us. And because of that, there probably won't be a lot of people around at the end. How can anyone connect to someone in denial? But we'll risk it because we are convinced that staying hidden and unknown is safer and less painful. It may feel freeing at times to wear masks and live in denial, but it is also imprisoning.

But there is something that can make the difference: God's love for us is unconditional. Because we have become so performance-based in everything, it is very hard to imagine someone—let alone God—loving us for who we are (whoever that is). And when we are loved unconditionally, the following is true: There is no truth in or about our lives that is so awful, painful and reprehensible that cannot be understood by God. I know, *I know* it sounds ridiculous. The love of God is very much like a light, a light that can shatter any darkness. It can shine through any mask. But most importantly, it can draw us out from both. There is something about it that makes us think about moving toward it.

But we have to understand one thing. Once we let God's light into our lives the truth becomes clearer. There is nothing so clarifying as the light of God's love. That is why so many of us stay home from church and stay away from God. Fear, judgment—we are wise to avoid these. But we are missing out on something else. What looks horrible and awful in the dark becomes comprehensible and hopeful in God's light and love. The disfigured face behind the mask becomes beautiful. This is the Gospel found in stories like *Beauty and the Beast.* The love of God walking the earth can find its way through the dark, beneath the mask to reach us unlike anything else.

The idea of being found, of being unmasked, is still terrifying. The truth will set us free, but will it also make us miserable? We get so used to hiding in the dark or behind masks that to come out from behind them is very uncomfortable—at first.

In Jesus's words, "If you continue in my word, you are truly my disciples; and you will know the truth and the truth shall set you free" (John 8:31–32). He is talking about two truths: The first is the truth that he is the messiah. The second one is about the truth of our lives.

For me, and I hope for all of us, it translates in this way: We will never heal, we will never even come close to being whole, and we will never be free until we acknowledge the truth of our lives. This is possible with the knowing that God searches for each one of us. He loves unconditionally and affirms doubting; he stands between us and stones.

It is only when we engage and inspect and accept the truth that we can begin to heal—but we don't have to do this alone. The alternate ending to a life of masks and strange light and darkness is being held by God and living in the truth.

The masks and the secrets can dissolve away revealing the truth of our lives, which is God's work still in progress— remember the reason and how he is making all things new. Darkness and denial and secrets can't stop it. The light of

God's love can shatter them, if we become brave enough to let it in. And in that light, we can begin to see the face that God lovingly sees—the face, the person—which is the possible, ultimate us.

## QUESTIONS

1. Can you think of some areas of your life about which you are in denial?

2. What do you think or feel when you hear the idea that what is horrible in our lives can become "comprehensible and hopeful" in God's light and love?

3. Can you think of some things to face the truth about as well as some things that need to be let go?

## Chapter 26

### A Second Chance Offers

# Release

## There is something else to hold onto.

"The dogmas of the quiet past are inadequate
to the stormy present."

—Abraham Lincoln

"What's past is prologue."

—William Shakespeare
*The Tempest*

Perhaps the hardest part of life is letting go. And one of the things that we hold onto most tightly—often with a clenched fist—is the past.

A lot of the suffocating anger we hold and carry is from decades ago. We can barely remember yesterday's news, but we can easily recall who said what to us years ago. Some people have anger from terrible events and wounds from the past. The anger is directed at themselves, at others, and at God. And the anger just sits and builds the wall higher and higher.

Somehow anger is a kind of memory-enhancer. That is part of the problem: If we could somehow forget, maybe we could let go.

Seeing that we don't have the technology yet to erase memory, there has to be another way, because this clenched fist is getting tired and this soul has virtually no spirit left.

The way it is going to go for those of us who are holding onto things like anger is not sunny. The health problems, the mental problems that can occur because of anger are many and almost inevitable. But there we are still holding on. Could we be holding onto the anger because it is all we have? Maybe we haven't found something to hold onto that we can we trust.

But we have to try. We need to remember a few things. There is hope as long as we have breath; there is always a chance—a chance to learn and to let go. While the walls around our souls seem soundproof, there still is one sound that can get through—God's voice calling our names. As great as our anger is, there is still something we long to hear, as much as we may deny it.

Beautiful words from the Bible that can easily be the words of God to us. "My beloved speaks and says to me, 'Arise, my love, my fair one, and come away; for now the winter is past, the rain is gone. The flowers appear on the earth; the time of singing has come, and the voice of the turtledove in our land...'" (Song of Solomon 2:10–12).

Imagine that: God calling us "beloved" and inviting us to arise and leave the winter of life behind. Why would we say no?

We would say "no" because it seems impossible. But it is tempting—and it is possible. Counseling may be in order, support groups might help, but there is only one thing in this world that can induce a healthy, healing sort of amnesia. That one thing is God's love as demonstrated in the purposeful grace that comes and finds us that says our name that invites us to let go of the past because he has something new. This love that is big enough and bold enough to cover and forget all offenses—available to each of us. There is a way to make it possible for a soul, for the first time in a while, to take a full deep breath—a holy breath. There is also a way for a clenched fist to slowly let go, unfold, and become an open hand willing to take God's hand. Both of these are possible, as we begin to forget why we were so angry.

## QUESTIONS

1.  Which parts of your past would you just love to let go?

    Why are you holding on to them?

2.  Is there anyway to let a clenched fist unfold and open?

    What are some ways this can start to happen?

3.  Do you ever think about how if we stay angry long enough we just might crash in a number of ways?

CHAPTER 27

A SECOND CHANCE OFFERS

# Restoration

## We have the technology—to rebuild souls and lives.

> "When you say a situation or a person is hopeless, you are slamming the door in the face of God."
> —Charles Allen

Almost everybody can remember the television show *The Six Million Dollar Man*. The story was that he was an astronaut and test-pilot who suffered a terrible crash during a test-flight. Obviously, most of us aren't astronauts, but we know a lot about crashing. Many of us don't get rescued from the crash immediately; nor are we aware of the technology for rebuilding our lives and souls. Long days are spent trying to recover from our crashes on our own.

The way things are going for many of us, there is little reason to hope. We have already given up, and we know how it is going to end. The poisons of sin and guilt are going to keep circulating in our systems until there is no body or soul left. The way we are going, many of us will end up a pile of dried up bones. And we have every right to feel this way—just look at where we are. All we have to do is take an honest look and we know where this is going.

Taking in the view, a lot of times it does look hopeless. But that's the thing: Hope is based on what we can't see.

No wonder we feel so hopeless. We are looking at what we *can* see.

If we only look at what can be seen, the only logical conclusion we can come to is that the world is going to hell—quickly. If our lives are a microcosm of the world, it feels the same and more personal. Families splitting apart, family members drowning in addictions—it's chaos and carnage. This view of life all hinges on one idea: that everything is random and that there is no plan or purpose.

No matter what the view is like, no matter how hopeless it may appear, we should remember that God is making all things new. And that sometimes to make things new, he has to wear away the surfaces of things, and us, to make them new.

How can we be sure? How can we trust that this is what is happening? How do we know there is, or is going to be, an alternate ending for us if we can't see it?

Well, there is a particular story in the Bible that would be a great special effects project for someone. The prophet Ezekiel is looking at this valley filled with dry bones (Ezekiel 37:1–14). And the Lord tells him it represents God's people. They had fallen away from God so much that all that was left was bones. In other words, they were dead both physically and spiritually. But the Lord tells Ezekiel to speak God's word to the bones, and they start to rattle and move and then come together to form bodies with flesh on them. But they needed breath, spirit. So again the Lord tells Ezekiel to speak God's word to them; and breath formed them into a huge army. Then the Lord tells Ezekiel that he was going to restore his people and bring them up from their graves.

It makes me think that with what we know about God through our box of Polaroids and stories like this, there is no such thing as hopeless when we are in God's hands.

We have also heard this truth in the stories of people we know. A friend of mine told me that when she would go to her AA meeting she could hardly believe the stories—stories of people who had homes and jobs and then a year later were living on the streets. In essence, they had become dried up bones. And yet God had an alternate ending for them. When you can go from being left for dead in the street all the way back to alive and hopeful and caring for others, it means that there is no person, no situation that is hopeless with God.

There is a way in which our dried bones can stand up again, regain muscle and flesh and be infused with breath, holy breath.

Like the *Six Million Dollar Man*, we can be rebuilt. The damage can be repaired—and we can be better, stronger, and faster than we were before.

## QUESTIONS

1. Can you believe that there is "technology" to rebuild souls and lives even from the worst crashes?

   Why or why not?

2. What about becoming even better than we were before?

   From where can this kind of hope come?

3. Can there be peace—real soulful peace—after crashes and storms? How?

## Chapter 28

### A Second Chance Offers

# Peace

## We will know God's peace when we are still.

"And I smiled to think God's greatness flowed around our
incompleteness, round our restlessness, His rest."
—Elizabeth Barrett Browning

"Who except God can give you peace?
Has the world ever been able to satisfy the heart?"
—Gerard Majella

We talk a lot about how things have changed. Life seems
faster; everyone is overbooked. At the same time, very few
of us are happy about it.

What is driving this pace? Well, a few things.

One of them is this idea of "never enough." Never
enough money, stuff, food, distraction, or entertainment.
And like a black hole, it just keeps sucking in more time
and things. Yet we feel emptier and emptier. This vicious
cycle keeps accelerating because the emptier we feel, the
more compelled we are to do and acquire more.

This accelerated motion of life also has to do with
pleasing others. It is related to "never enough" in some ways.
For example, there is never enough we can do to please
ourselves but also spouses, family members, employers.
Many times, I've had conversations with women who are the

caretakers of their families, and they talk about how they are pleasing everyone else, leaving nothing for themselves. It is a dangerous way of operating; and so many of us do this. It may be well intentioned, but it will leave us empty.

One more reason we are running around like crazy is that we are hiding. Many of us think that if we keep ourselves so busy, we don't have to be home or at our desk or wherever we are trying to avoid. It is actually an effective short-term strategy. If we are so busy, we don't have to talk about anything—we don't have time, right? This desire to hide from the truth of our lives or from what God may be saying is strong. It keeps us moving; not necessarily toward a destination—just away.

This hiding, the pleasing others and chasing things and people to fill the void might work for a while. But if we are doing these things for some kind of peace, like I think we are, we will never have it this way.

One way to think about our fast-paced lives is how we can never experience the peace of being in the palm of God's hand if we are moving. Here's God trying to keep us contained in his palm and we are always trying to run and jump off. We don't know God's peace because we can never stay still.

And then there are these words from the Bible, "Be still and know that I am God!" (Psalm 46:10). Perhaps a lot of the time we have been wondering where God has been, we couldn't feel his presence because we weren't being still.

Doesn't it make sense? Of course God's presence is always there. What changes is our ability to experience it. So that if we are always distracted and seeking other things, pleasing others and hiding, our ability to sense God's peace suffers.

Can any of us even remember what it is like to be still? Remember lying in the grass and watching clouds form and move? When was the last time we stopped and felt and listened to ourselves breathe? Go ahead, try it!

See, I think we can remember it. But we also fear it. If we are still, stuff won't get done, right? But really, what won't get done is this alternate ending for our lives.

Picture this—pressing the pause button. The drive to do and get and please and hide just stops. There is just us, breathing, praying maybe, putting all the other crazy thoughts out of our minds. And then in that moment we can sense just the hint of something new—the peace of God.

## QUESTIONS

1. What is causing this rapid increase in the pace of life?

   How do you see it affecting your life?


2. Can you think of a time when you felt peaceful inside?

   What was unique about it?


3. Do you ever think that if everything would just slow down, you could deal with some other things like healing?

CHAPTER 29

A SECOND CHANCE OFFERS

# Sensation

## Healing starts with a reach.

"Daughter, you took a risk of faith,
and now you're healed and whole.
Live well, live blessed! Be healed of your plague."
—Mark 5:34
*The Message*

It makes sense that most of us don't know what healing feels like, because we can't even say we are hurt. Why do we choose numbness over even the chance of healing? It could be a status quo thing. Healing might mean dealing with the truth, and that might bring more misery at first.

In other words, the pain we know is better than the healing we don't, or something like that. But isn't there also a point where we get tired of crying out from the depths and being locked in a prison?

The isolation is so hard. Even with so many people in this world and around us, we can still be so alone. It's the isolation that comes from nobody understanding. Let's face it, most people don't want to join us in the depths. This is why it is so lonely and difficult when we are grieving. Being out of touch or untouchable from the depths, we get used to be alone and having little to no real contact. This is where the numbing comes in—whether naturally or with assistance. When we get used to not feeling anything, somehow it *feels* better. But with crying out from the depths, we have to maintain the anesthesia, so to speak.

And that is how the finale is determined for so many. A numbed, disconnected—yet smiling (pretending there is nothing wrong)—ending. No connections with people, with God, with anything. It is the very definition of a tragedy. Whether we are crying out from the depths or imprisoned, it may not get worse, but it certainly will not get better. Unless ...

There is this story in the Bible about a woman who needed healing (Mark 5:24–34). She had been suffering with a terrible and embarrassing condition for twelve years. She went to many doctors and spent all her money, but the condition only worsened. I think about how so many of us may not have her "condition," but certainly we have struggled and suffered with a number of afflictions for twelve years or more.

The woman heard about Jesus and went in search of him, despite religious rules and fear; she reached out for him believing that, "If I but touch his cloak, I will be made well" (Mark 5:28). Upon touching Jesus, she was healed. But she disappeared into the crowd again, hoping to go back to hiding. She was still ashamed and wanting to live in the shadows. Even though the disease was gone, she was not yet whole. Jesus called out to her until she returned and fell down in front of him. When she admitted that she touched his cloak, Jesus declared her fully healed—body *and* soul.

She, like us, had suffered for years. She had cried out from the depths for years. She was imprisoned for years. She had no connections, and she was at the end of her rope. But she did that one thing, took that one risk ... .

I know that when I have been at the end of the rope, I fought taking that risk. Either I thought I didn't need help, or I thought that I was being a wimp for needing help.

Either way, I was wrong. And when I finally reached out, God and others were there—right there.

For example, after my Mom died, I sensed that there were many deep issues that were beyond my ability to deal with. But the thought of going to a counselor for help made me feel like a baby. But after some encouragement and prayer, I called a guy and went to counseling for about six months. It was one of the best things I ever did.

Contrary to popular, self-help thinking, we can't heal ourselves. It wasn't the design. And it's not a matter of being weak or incapable. God designed us to depend on him and to be connected in healthy ways to other human beings.

And that is why the healing won't begin until we acknowledge that the hurt is real and then begin to draw it out. Author John Bradshaw writes that healing begins with externalizing the disease or condition.[1]

What does healing feel like? It's like reaching out and grabbing hold of a cloak or a hand. What does healing feel like? It is the return of sensation of feeling. Healing is when the numbness begins to diminish and there is a tingle again of pain or joy—mostly pain at first—telling us that the healing has started.

The prisoners may not be able to reach far, but it is far enough to stretch a hand through the bars. I know it may feel like miles, I know it hasn't worked before, and I know it is scary, but just the reach can begin the healing. We can feel something again.

## QUESTIONS

1. What are the broken and wounded places and parts of your life that are in need of healing?

   Do you see any patterns or connections?

2. What would it be like to be whole again or just to feel pain or joy?

   What would be different than now?

3. What would it be like to start to feel enough so that tears flow again?

# CHAPTER 30

## A SECOND CHANCE OFFERS

# Renewal

## Something wonderful through the tears.

"When you reach the place of tears, then know that your spirit has come out of the prison of this world and has set its foot upon the path that leads towards the new age."
—St. John Climacus

There are a bunch of things in this world that are so numerous they can barely be counted—just estimated at best. Things like blueberries (personal favorite), leaves, and grains of sand. Something that fits in this category that is a little closer to the heart is tears. How many tears have we cried in our lifetimes? How do we even begin to count?

We don't remember tears as much as why we have cried. We have talked about crying out from the depths. There are the tears that have flowed from emergency rooms and from funerals. Crying out for God—or anybody—to hear us, to know our tears. There is something about tears and silence, because we so often want to cry alone. On the other hand, we are often crying all the more because we are alone.

But what about when we are crying and there are no tears? I wish there was a special lens, like night vision, that I could use to see people's tears when they aren't literally crying. Because I know it is happening all the time. Some days I can see it—and people avoid me because they don't want to talk about it. A lot of us get to that point. I don't know about the physiological truth of that—that the tear ducts can actually be emptied. But I have listened and seen enough to know it's true.

Remember that phrase, "If a tree falls in the forest, does anyone know?" Likewise, if tears fall from someone inside a prison, does anyone know? Probably not. I guess with the forest, we can only know if we see the tree down. Same thing for people in prisons. We only know their tears or pain when they collapse or break down or die.

And when I say prison, it can mean an actual correctional institute. But it also means the person wandering the mall and the woman sitting down the pew from you or the quiet neighbor who only comes out to get the paper. Many times a prison doesn't have bars.

We could just keep going on in our grief and our prisons, but the tears would become so numerous that we would be swimming in them, drowning. Think about that—drowning in our own tears. How sad does that sound? There is a verse from the Bible that says, "My tears have been my food day and night, while people say to me continually, 'Where is your God'" (Psalm 42:3). Yuck! And yet that is the meal plan and the future for so many.

But then I think of the guy Bart who encounters Jesus and is asked, "What do you want?" All the tears Bart must have cried after he lost his sight and was tossed to the side of the road of life. He was in the prison of his disability and grief as well as a society-imposed one, as many are today. And yet, we are reminded to expect the unexpected—to be prepared to tell God what we want ... and to sometimes receive it.

Then I think of how we said before that an authentic gathering of believers can be like heaven on earth. And that in that place, amazing, amazing things can happen— miracles even. Things like reconciliation and healing. Things like having our hands held as we cry. Things like a hand reaching into our prison to hold our hands; or being invited out of our prisons.

Still, there is no promise from God that here in this life the tears will end. "Hearts will never be practical until they are made unbreakable," the Wizard tells the Tin Man in the *Wizard of Oz.*

But, then imagine this from God's new age to come, "See, the home of God is among mortals. He will dwell with them; they will be his peoples, and God himself will be with them; he will wipe every tear from their eyes. Death will be no more; mourning and crying and pain will be no more, for the first things have passed away" (Revelation 21:3–4).

Doesn't it mean that if God is going to wipe every tear from our eyes that he has to be tracking and counting them all? Is he is aware—there—each time we weep? And if our tears count, then certainly we count in the eyes of the Father? I'm just saying...

It's possible for the same hand that reaches through the prison bars to wipe away "every tear from our eyes." It's possible that the same hand that holds us in its palm will wipe away our tears of salt and water at funerals. The same hand works through years and sins and miles to baptize us with water and the Spirit. So that what was supposed to be a funeral can become a baptism.

## QUESTIONS

1.  What does it say about God's character if he is counting our tears and will wipe them all away?

2.  Since there is no promise of "no tears" in this life, could this God counting tears be the next best thing?

    Please say some more about that.

3.  Through the tears, have you ever hoped Jesus was really, actually there?

## CHAPTER 31

### A SECOND CHANCE OFFERS

# Faith

"Jesus, is that you?"

"Our old history ends with the cross;
our new history begins with the resurrection."
—Watchman Nee

I remember waking up one Easter morning and hearing a noise out in the living room. As an eight year old, I knew it must be Jesus. Everybody else was asleep, so I crept out of my bedroom, and as I turned the corner, I scanned the living room and said quietly, "Jesus, is that you?"

Jesus was not visibly there. It was the empty living room. But I remember believing that he might be there, wanting him there. I understood enough to know that Jesus was real and that it might be possible that he could be in my living room on Easter morning. That story has all the ingredients of genuine faith. It has an earnest, fearless desire to meet God as well as blind faith—a sense of possibility. This is what we lose as adults and have to find again somehow. Part of why I was able to think that way then was my young age. Skeptics would say I didn't know any better; I hadn't learned the ways of the world yet. But I remember it vividly now for a reason: because it was pure and wonderful. It didn't matter that he wasn't there for me to see. It was much more about the reach of my little heart.

In the actual Easter story, two women go to Jesus's tomb (Luke 24:1–11). They were going there with spices to ritually anoint Jesus's buried body. Even though they knew he had said he would rise, they clearly were going to the tomb, where they thought he was, thinking he was dead and gone. Further, they were operating as if he wasn't who he claimed he was—not a savior but just a kind teacher and friend.

And if things hadn't been otherwise, they would have anointed his body and grieved. They would have remembered him fondly and tried to practice what he preached. Maybe they would return to the tomb from time to time for comfort. Their lives would be better for having known him, but that would be about it.

Sadly, that reminds me of how many people have experienced faith and worship at some point in their lives. It can seem like going to a tomb out of a sense of ritual or habit expecting nothing more than a dead Jesus whom people love and thinking that is all that is required or possible.

What kind of story has an ending like that? Okay, I'll say it: a tragedy. A tragedy is when something terrible happens despite much potential and possibility.

Another ending is possible through God making all things new. Let's go back to the story of the women going to Jesus's tomb. When they arrive at the tomb, they find that the stone door to the chamber is moved and open. They go in and find the body is not there. Two messengers for God are there instead. The women throw themselves down in fear. And the messengers ask a most penetrating question. "Why do you look for the living among the dead? He is not here, but has risen" (Luke 24:5). They remind the women that Jesus said he would rise again and the women leave to tell others that Jesus is alive.

Now if that isn't a great worship service and sermon, I don't know what is! The women experience God's presence via the messengers; they are challenged with a question; they are reminded of Jesus's words; they remember and claim them; then they go out and tell people about it. This is the ending, this is the life God is offering to us.

What we want and what we need is to be able to wake up each Sunday morning and expect Jesus to be in the living room and in the sanctuary. It's about resurrecting believers from the dead. It's about believing that even the impossible can happen. It's about believing there was a day long ago when the ultimate alternate ending happened and understanding how it brings life from death right now. It was the alternate ending that makes all other alternate endings possible.

There may be nothing like a Sunday morning in America. But even better, there is absolutely nothing like living, worshipping, and serving as if every Sunday in America was more than just another Sunday—but Easter Sunday.

There is a way to live every day with the same wonder, awe, surprise, and joy of Easter morning. There is a way to look for and find the living Jesus among living people. There is a way to live in the light and the power of resurrection.

## QUESTIONS

1. What would it take for you to believe in the possibility of Jesus being in the room?

2. Can we live and believe like it's Easter Sunday every week?

   Why or why not?

3. What do you think church has done to get in the way of authentic faith and seeing Jesus clearly?

CHAPTER 32

A SECOND CHANCE OFFERS

# Vision

## To see and sense God's presence again and again.

"God makes of all things mysteries and sacraments of love, why should not every moment of our lives be a sort of communion with the divine love?"
—Jean-Pierre de Causssade

Isn't it amazing when we first open our eyes in the morning? That first glimpse is fuzzy, but there is light. And then on our own, or with some help from glasses, our sight corrects and clarifies, and we can see again. But think about how before that, our eyes were closed and we didn't see.

Remember those posters from a few years ago that when you looked at them it just looked like this random mix of colors and circles and other shapes? We were supposed look at it for a while and then suddenly see a word or phrase.

Sight is complex. We can be looking at something and seeing things all the time and not really "see" what they are. This happens with faith too. It could be routine, it could be a purposeful blindness or turning away, but at some point, we can't see what faith is about. We can lip sync the words, we can smile on cue, remember the stories, but we just can't see it.

How many times have we walked into church and even the cross or crucifix just fades to the point where we don't see them anymore? There are so many times when we don't even see people crying next to us in the pew. There is a terrible blindness in the very place of faith.

It's a kind of living in the dark, though it's light. There is something almost twisted about phrases like "blind faith" and "we walk by faith and not by sight" (2 Corinthians 5:7). It seems like a sick joke to be told that if we have real faith it is something we can't see. Or is there something else about this ... ?

With everything so visual today, one would think there would be a way to make faith and God more visible through some kind of screen technology. Not happening. So we just kind of stumble through this life, bouncing off walls in this blurred inconsistent light, blinded by life and ourselves.

One story goes that these two guys were walking down the road of defeat and grief (Luke 24:13–32). A stranger approached them. As their teacher had taught them, everybody was their neighbor, so they welcomed the man and asked him to join them. Along the journey, the wise and mysterious stranger comforted them and taught them many things. When they reached a certain point, they invited him to stay with them for dinner.

When they sat down together, the stranger began the meal by breaking the bread, just like their teacher before he was killed. And just as the stranger gave thanks and broke the bread, he revealed that he was the teacher, Jesus, all along. In that moment, that holy and sacred moment, the risen one was visible—more than visible: they were in his very presence.

To be in his presence. That is what faith and worship and life were meant to be. In this story we see that the two disciples were at the end of their rope. And Jesus met them where they were. He came along beside them. As much as we have talked about not being recognized by God, here the disciples who knew him so well did not recognize him; they were so blinded by grief and despair.

These disciples had once believed and then had given up on Jesus. They were running away, their faith shattered. And yet he came to them on that road, walked with them, and shared the sacred meal with them. Might this mean that anyone today with a penitent heart can be welcomed at the Lord's table to share in the communion with his body and blood? Jesus himself does not appear to draw a line here.

The sacrament of the Lord's Supper, no matter what you believe or how you celebrate it, is about being literally connected with Jesus's presence. And the one thing about it is that we can't do it alone. It is most often done in community; but even when it happens in a hospital or living room it is still offered by another.

What we all love about communion is that it is a sacred experience. That is what we miss about it when we have been away from it for so long. Perhaps more than any other activity at church, the Lord's Supper or communion is that experience that is the most sacred. There is something pure about it. Prayers, readings, and sermons come and go. But the Lord's supper engages the senses in a very different way. It is not anybody's opinion on Scripture or fumbled words in prayer. We hear the words; we see the bread and the cup; we smell, taste and feel them. And sometimes, when we can come close to understanding the depth and the meaning of it all, we can enter into his presence—a sixth sense, so to speak. That is what is sacred and miraculous about it. "The spiritual virtue of a sacrament is like light; although it passes among the impure, it is not polluted," said Augustine.

From being held in the palm of his hand to holding communion with the body of Christ in *our* hands is one of those things that makes this faith thing seem a little more real than usual.

To be in God's presence, to feel a part of him, is what we long for. We may not have thought of it that way in a long time (or ever for that matter). But it is the way we were designed. To see and experience the grace and presence of God.

Our sight can be restored and our blindness can be healed when we are able to focus on Jesus alone. That is why communion is so wonderful. It is because, for a moment with that bread and cup, we aren't focused on ourselves, the church, anything else—except the body and the blood.

And it is in that holy and sacred moment when our eyes can open ...

## QUESTIONS

1.  Do you long for a sacramental experience with Christ?

    Does a part of you long to feel his presence—even as impossible as it may seem?

2.  What are some of the causes of our own blindness when it comes to seeing God?

3.  What is it about the bread and the cup, the body and the blood, that is more real than anything else we experience in faith?

## CHAPTER 33

A SECOND CHANCE OFFERS

# Something Real

## The power beneath the surface and within us.

"The soul is more honorable than the substance of the
body; seeing that it is God's image and inspiration."
—Cyril of Alexandria

We spend a lot of time thinking and talking about the
ugly "stuff" inside of us. And we blame our parents or our
pasts. The blaming doesn't really change anything, but the
understanding can be helpful.

One part of the ugly "stuff" inside us is this need that we
can't seem to satisfy—the "never enough."

Another part is this poison of sin and guilt coursing
through our veins that keeps building up, our toxicity levels
increasing. It's just all in there and there doesn't seem to be
a way to remove it, or at least reduce it.

On top of all this there is the fear of being loved and the
fear of not being loved. Fear pulls like gravity on our lives,
making us feel powerless. With fear holding us down, we
don't dare, we don't try new things.

This is where most of us are and unfortunately where
we'll stay. The way this story is going—between there never
being enough, the poison, and the fear—we are destined
for misery. It will be predictable; nothing much will happen.
The usual life events will slowly chip away at us, but nothing
extraordinary. Ours is the kind of desperation that is rarely

known or heard except within the confines of our souls and occasionally in prayers.

But in that desperation—from the end of the rope—we can glimpse and get an idea of that which cannot be seen. This idea is that the things that are invisible and eternal are what really matter and what really have value.

At the same time, we remember from the box of Polaroids, this portrait of how doubts draw us closer to God. Dealing with doubts leads us closer to God and further inside ourselves.

We also realize that in the face of our fears, God loves us in a way that removes fear. This "real" love of God is designed to surpass and swallow all fears. It is a love that is inside, not outside.

Think of the *possibilities* inside us: "The spirit of him who raised Jesus from the dead is living in you, he who raised Christ from the dead will also give life to your mortal bodies through the Spirit" (Romans 8:11).

Jesus rose from the dead, and the power that accomplished that is inside us? What could this mean?

It could mean that all the "stuff" inside us, though quite devastating and real, can be overcome by the power of resurrection. The very act of resurrection is bringing life from death. It is also bringing satisfaction from hunger, strength from poison, power from weakness, and release from fear.

To imagine the possibilities, the alternate endings with this power within us. This life doesn't have to end in desperation. Think about trusting in and leaning on this power within us, beyond us, enabling us to turn to God and turn inside for soul satisfaction; enabling us to reverse the effects of the poison of sin and guilt within us. There is a way.

## QUESTIONS

1. Is it possible the same Spirit that raised Christ from the dead is transforming us from the inside?

   Or should we say, isn't it possible, if this is true?

2. What does it mean for our living, if we can't outrun or remove the Holy Spirit from our souls?

3. Can this power within us even help us overcome or withstand the expectations and judgments of others?

CHAPTER 34

A SECOND CHANCE OFFERS

# Grace

## There is no sin or lifetime of sin bigger than God.

"Forgiveness is the answer to the child's dream of a miracle by which what is broken is made whole again, what is soiled is again made clean."
—Dag Hammarskjold

There are many ways to die, but can we die or be killed by … measurement? Not literally with a ruler or tape measure, of course. No, I am talking about death by the slow, gradual, soul-compressing force of expectations, judgments, and failures.

We have talked about how these things send us to, and keep us at, the rope end. For example, we have talked about how stones and frowns not only hurt, but also leave us with few choices. We can choose to live up to others' expectations and to live by avoiding judgments and never have our own life—always living for someone else. Sometimes it's our parents, spouses, pastors and priests, church members—but there always seems to be a someone else.

We also face this constant highlight reel of our failures, whether we are producing it ourselves or various people in our lives insist on syndicating it and running it over and over. Another destructive element of the failure highlight film is that we come to believe, or are taught, or are left to believe, that God is also a fan. We can't help but come to see God as a nit-picking, perfection-demanding old codger who we have never, can never, and will never please.

Many of us start and end the day thinking like this. From the moment we wake, we know that we are not going to be able to please anybody. Often the way it plays out in our minds and in our lives is that we are unforgiven, that nothing we do or have done can be enough or is beyond repair. We have exceeded the sin and mistake limit. We are reminded over and over how we failed or how we broke something and how there is no fixing it.

The most confusing part may be when we have been told we are forgiven but aren't treated like that. And then when we go to church and hear we are forgiven. It grieves me when, as a pastor, I offer "Words of Assurance" that express God's forgiveness in Jesus, I know that many people gathered heard the words but believe they don't apply to them.

Instead, what so many people believe applies to them are the lines, the rules, the regulations. This is not to say that the lines are not important or real—they are. But it is how we view them and how they are imposed on us that make all the difference.

Even so, the lines are drawn; the box—more like a coffin—is built, and we are placed in it long before we stop breathing. And this is how it begins to end for so many of us. It's a kind of death by the measurements and expectations and failures closing in on us until we can barely move or breathe anymore.

But there is another way. It doesn't have to end like that. We remember the fading Polaroid of God's real love that is unconditional. It is given freely. We don't have to earn it. It has already been done at the cross. As evangelist John Stott said, "The symbol of the religion of Jesus is the cross, not the scales."[1] This is the love that stands between us and stones, between us and the scales, between us and death.

Because of God's love, it is *never* too late, not just because of its nature but also because of how God is constantly working for our good—no matter how it seems. Though we may be in a coffin, if we are still breathing, there still is a chance for us; the do-over doesn't expire until we do. Therefore it is never too late to feel forgiven or forgive.

There is a reunion story in the Bible that exceeds that of any Oprah show. It is the reunion between Joseph and his brothers (Genesis 37–45). These are same brothers that threw him in a ditch and sold him into slavery because of their jealousy. Years later they are in Egypt (where Joseph has become a governor-like official) begging for food because of a famine. Joseph knows who they are, but they don't recognize him. And he even tries to trick and punish them, but he can't go through with it.

"So Joseph said to his brothers, 'Come near to me, I pray you.' And they came near. And he said, 'I am your brother Joseph, whom you sold into Egypt. And now do not be distressed, or angry with yourselves, because you sold me here; for God sent me before you to preserve life'" (Genesis 45:4–5).

But isn't Joseph supposed to take revenge on them, Rambo-style? Isn't he supposed to start throwing chairs? How is Joseph able to forgive this terrible act and grant his brothers alternate ending? It isn't because he is a nice guy or because he has a bad memory. There is something else. It's because he trusted in the Lord, because he appreciated the second chances from God and because he was able to glimpse that God had a bigger picture in mind. A picture that no sin, no act of hatred or neglect could derail. Joseph's actions, forgiving on God's power, opened an alternate ending for himself and his family.

Here's what they didn't tell us: There is no sin or lifetime of sin that is bigger than God. We believe our sins or those of others have the ability to alter God's plans for us and this world. We have given sin much more power than it has. If God is omnipresent, omnipotent, and omniscient, there is nothing beyond him. Sin is of this world—no matter how devastating or widespread—and is under God's authority. The miracle is that sins are not greater than God's grace. Jesus's work on the cross made it so that no matter how many sins and failures we pile up, the sum total will always be less than God's grace.

We have tried so many times before to forgive ourselves as well as to forgive others on our own power. Neither can be done without God's help.

There was a church in New Jersey that held a reconciliation service a few years ago. A member, who was the treasurer, had stolen about $35,000 over a few years. The member was caught and faced criminal penalties. But the leadership of that church held a service where the member asked for forgiveness and the members offered it accompanied by Scripture and music about reconciliation.

It was a little bit of heaven on earth. Something like this is only possible by the grace of God. Left to our human ways, we want to punish and judge and expel, right? "Humanity is never so beautiful as when praying for forgiveness or else forgiving another,"[2] wrote German writer Jean Paul Richter. Why is this true? Because when we pray for God's grace for ourselves or rely on it to forgive others, we are acknowledging our need for and inviting the love of God into our hearts and to the situations of life.

There is a way to do this, to never worry again about being good enough, smart enough, and lovable enough; a way to finally archive and forget about the failure highlight films. It's a way to live in the freedom of God's grace; to not only be forgiven, but feel and live forgiven, and then to forgive others.

## QUESTIONS

1. Have you ever thought that God's forgiveness doesn't apply to you?

   From where did that thought come—can you remember being told or taught that?

2. Do you feel the expectations and measurements closing in on you?

   What can you do about them?

3. Could living forgiven and forgiving others be an untapped source of joy in your life?

# CHAPTER 35

## A SECOND CHANCE OFFERS

# Joy

## God doesn't want you to be happy ... He wants you to have joy. There is a difference.

"Happiness depends on what happens; joy does not."
—Oswald Chambers

Some of us have lived so long with tears and emptiness, that we don't even notice them anymore. They are like the wallpaper; they just blend into the background of our lives. Many times, to deal with the tears and emptiness we start to do destructive things. We have done a lot of damage to ourselves and others in an effort to stop the tears and fill the emptiness.

"Men cannot live without joy; therefore when he is deprived of true spiritual joys it is necessary that he become addicted to carnal pleasures,"[1] wrote theologian Thomas Aquinas. In our terms today, he is basically saying that we as humans, one way or another are going to get our "happy" on. The design was for us to employ "spiritual joys" for our fulfillment. But instead, we get sidetracked or distracted or turned around.

And so the chase begins. "I just want you to be happy." How many times have we heard that? How many times have we said to ourselves, "I just want to be happy?" But I thought, "the one who dies with the most toys wins" right? Except that the one with most toys usually has the least joy. Who

will be the king or queen of the self-storage places? We try
buying happiness, squeezing happiness from relationships,
and manufacturing happiness from a new job.

We have sought joy and ended up with misery. How many
plans and schemes to bring about happiness—ones that
may have at first succeeded—turn to permanent states of
despair? So much of our despair is not from circumstance
and events but from our own pursuits.

So where does joy come from? "May those who sow in
tears reap with shouts of joy. Those who go out weeping,
bearing the seed for sowing, shall come home with shouts
of joy, carrying their sheaves" (Psalm 126:5–6). What is in
the tears that can yield shouts of joy? It is our need for God.
Whether we are crying out from the depths or from our
prisons—we are crying out for God's help.

Let's think about our best dreams, the ones we haven't
given up on … yet. When did those best dreams appear? If
we can recall, it is usually out of the seeds of the worst times.
They come from the times when we were forced to pray the
most outrageous prayers. Prayers and cries from the end of
the rope. These are the dreams and prayers from when we
thought nothing was possible.

Could God be that good so as to make it so that it is never
too late for joy? Could God be that good as to never stop
making all things new no matter how old or damaged they
are? This is what the fading Polaroids seemed to show.

"The religion of Christ is the religion of joy. Christ came
to take away our sins, to roll off our curse, to unbind our
chains, to open our prison house, to cancel our debt …
Is not this joy? Where can we find a joy so real, so deep,
so pure, so lasting," wrote renowned preacher Octavius
Winslow. [2]

Joy coming from tears and emptiness? We are so
programmed to think the opposite. The formula for
happiness is this: Find something or someone you like, hold

onto it, and make it work for as long as you can; then move on to the next happy thing. But it's God's way to bring joy out of tears. Here's why: It reveals that joy is completely from God when it comes from tears and emptiness rather than stuff. It is no coincidence that from the times we need God most—at the rope ends—come the seeds, dreams, and ultimately realities of joy.

See, happiness is a good day. Happiness is opening a gift. In other words, they both come to an end. Days come and go. The wrapping gets thrown away and the gift gets forgotten after a while. But joy is what we didn't think could happen. Joy is the dawn breaking from a long night of sorrow. Joy is knowing that God gives do-overs. Happiness is about the body; joy is about the soul. We all know which one is going to last.

We all have heard of leaps of faith. It's when you jump out stretching for something with a belief and no safety net. This alternate ending is a leap of joy. And it takes two steps. First it is leaping away from making our own happiness, leaping away from fear, failure, pain, and tears. It is a letting go of all the things of this world that appear to give us pleasure. Second, as we are letting go of these things of the world, it is a leap and reach towards living every day believing that God *is* that good.

And so, it is possible to find and experience real joy in this world—beyond self-storage units and stuff. There is a way for dreams and joy to be distilled from all the tears and emptiness. There is a way to find joy in this life, real and lasting joy.

# QUESTIONS

1.  Do you believe that happiness is what life is all about?

    In other words, is the goal just to squeeze out some happiness from life?

2.  Can you see a difference between happiness and joy?

    Please share how you see the difference.

3.  Could there be any more joy than in an unexpected return or homecoming?

    Could you share any personal experiences along these lines?

CHAPTER 36

A SECOND CHANCE OFFERS

# A Homecoming

### He could come home after all, because he came home first in his heart.

"He who counts the stars and calls them by their names
is in no danger of forgetting His own children."
—C.H. Spurgeon

It was a familiar ending. It seemed inevitable. This son, this brother had gone off, thinking he knew better.[1] He thought he was too big for his family, for his hometown. So he took his share of the family fortune and left. He would show them.

Well, things didn't go exactly as planned. They never do. The world kind of got in the way of the plans. The distractions, the pleasure-chasing, all the wasted time on fruitless adventures—they ate up that portion of the family fortune rather quickly.

"No problem," this son and brother thought. He would just get a job and build everything from there. But the job was worse than dead-end. And there he was—everything was lost and he was a prisoner of his choices and the consequences of those choices. He had reached the end of his rope. And like we have said, there is a certain clarity at the rope end. And a crazy idea came to him, that maybe he could go back to his father and ask for forgiveness.

It's amazing how the rope end influences us to conceive of the impossible things we swore we never would do. We start thinking about things that only happen in dreams. We start facing the truth at the rope end. At the same time, it's incredible how the end of the rope jars our memories of good things like old pictures of what was good—of what can still be good.

Here was this son and brother, hitting the bottom; how far he had fallen. It all could have ended right there. Maybe he wouldn't die right away, but his soul was nearly dead, and he was already lost to his family. It could have been a familiar ending; one we have read and heard about so many times … .

But he was on his way back. *It couldn't get any worse*, he must have thought. Facing a living or an actual hell or facing his father: His father might forgive him, but hell wouldn't. He practiced his speech again. The distance and the walking weren't as far as the distance he felt from his father. It could have been a million miles, but the gulf he felt between his family and himself was much more. The shame, the sense of failure, the sins and the damage were all wider and farther than any road.

So many questions. *Will he recognize or remember me? Will they let me back into the family?* He kept walking despite the prison he was carrying, despite the fear, despite the doubt.

And then it was in sight. The house—and the family he had shamed and failed. He practiced the speech again. "Father, I have sinned against you … I am not worthy to be your son … ." The road was the same and as he looked up he could see someone moving toward him, now running. It was his father.

*Can I do this?* the son asked himself. *Maybe I should turn and run; this feels awful, I think I am going to be sick*, he thought. *He is probably running towards me to tell me to get out of here; that I am not allowed to come near this house ever again.*

The son remembered a chasing game they used to play when he and his brother were children. The father would chase them from far away. And as he would run after the sons, he looked bigger and bigger to them as he approached. He always looked larger and clearer just as he scooped them up in his strong arms.

Now the father was running toward the son again. The once impossible distance was now rapidly disappearing. The father was coming from his house—the son coming from the rope end. And just like before, the father became bigger as he came closer.

The son looked down as if to hide. And when he looked up again the father was there right in front of him his arms first raising and then opening ... opening for an embrace.

*He wants to hug me?* the son thought in confusion. And then it happened: The son was in the arms of the father again. The father embraced and kissed the son.

And all the son could think was, *I don't deserve this, I am not worthy of this man's embraces and kisses.* He thought of his speech. *I have to say my speech about how I am not worthy.*

He tried to stammer out the words, but then he realized that his father wasn't listening; his father was already starting to organize the party. What about the punishment? What about the condemnation? What about the speech about awful he was?

See, the return itself spoke volumes more than any speech or confession. He could come home after all, because he came home first in his heart. Before he even took the first step with his foot, he was already home. The miles, the distance, and the sins were miraculously bridged with that one change and lurch and tilt of his heart.

After all—for the son and for us—there is an open seat. We can be recognized; we can be found, heard and held. After all, our souls can breathe again, the eclipse can pass, and there can be real fulfillment. After all, the prison door can open and the questions can be answered. After all, for the son and for us, it can be like this and more by returning through the broken pieces of our hearts.

After all, the celebration can begin.

## QUESTIONS

1. Have you been or have you ever tried to make it on your own and failed?

2. Is there any chance God could be like the father in this story?

   Why or why not?

3. Could you also come home to God in your heart before you even take a step?

   Are you ready to do this by asking for a second chance?

# THE SECOND CHANCE

"Years of repentance are necessary in order
to blot out a sin in the eyes of men,
but one tear of repentance suffices for God."
—French Proverb

Yes, the celebration for the son and for us can begin. According to Jesus, the celebration in heaven for the same thing actually begins before the one here (Luke 15:7). Here it started when the son came home and was embraced by the father. But the trip home and the celebration began when the son, at the end of his rope, did just one thing. "So he set off and went to his father" (Luke 15:20). Everything was in that one movement, this one motion, starting with the heart—the way to all alternate endings for us.

The truth is that we are never so far away from being found. Pride delays it, denial hides it, anger pushes it away; but we get found at the end of the rope because it is where we finally come to see the truth—that we are lost without God. We also see the things that get in the way—religion, people who judge us and ourselves—for what they are. The experience of the rope end is real; and we can't have an alternate ending without a rope end. The paths to alternate endings are glimpsed in the emerging clarity of the rope end. There is no other way to find them. It is as if they only exist, by design, from the "portal" of the rope end. This is why it is so harmful to keep numbing and denying—nothing will ever change in that state. And yes, maybe it won't be as painful as acknowledging the truth, reaching out, and healing—but it is not, and never will be, living.

Hanging and swinging from the end of the rope, we are stripped of our defenses, pretenses, and facades. It is just us and God at the rope end. It is what we talked about before—about God making everything new—when restoring something, the old has to be worn away first.

For me, at my worst rope end, I hit bottom. Everything I cared about, cherished, and enjoyed was gone. It was just me, or so I thought. I had known God all my life. I had gone through the rituals and motions. But all of that, and my friends, and my ways of solving problems were all stripped away. I walked around aimlessly for hours, barely held onto a part-time job, and watched helplessly as a lot of things around me unraveled. It was pure rope end. That was when the only thing I had left was to start imagining myself in the palm of God's hand. I was breaking and full of pain and anguish and shame. I felt like a complete failure. All my promise and potential was a lie and was worthless now. But ...

But it was also the first time that I felt the need for a savior, my savior. And oh how I needed him. It was also the first time I started saying real prayers, not just rote, routine ones. It was the first time I started dreaming impossible dreams and believing that someday, by God's hand, they would come true. In addition, I stopped going to church and instead walked to my favorite park, carrying my Bible and some white bread and grape juice so I could worship God for real. And I sat in a spot in the park and worshipped God purely. I was reading Scripture, praying, feeling God's presence, remembering the Last Supper. It was about desire rather than habit; it was about the heart rather than obligation. All of these things I would never have done if it weren't for being allowed to purposefully and gently sink to the rope end. And now, how can I not thank God for it? True, I couldn't say it then or even understand it. All along, God was carefully stripping away my pride and self-sufficiency and self-righteousness and anything in which I had falsely put my trust. And have there been more rope ends since that first one? Yes, many. Because the restoration work keeps going—it's never fully done. But without the rope end, there would have been no alternate ending for me and for many others.

As shocking as this sounds, our times at the end of the rope are part of the plan—God's plan to return us to him not through magic or a blinking of the eyes but in and through and around our sins and failures and mistakes. As awful as they are, rope ends, past, present and future, are part of God's purpose—his purpose of redeeming us through Jesus's work on the cross and resurrection. And this is a central part of the loving character of God. If God can do anything, why does he choose to accomplish our return by way of the rope end? Because we are his children and he values us that much that he waits for us to claim or reclaim him in the rope ends, valleys, and depths—when it will be authentic. Not in the religious pantomime and phoniness and feel-good stuff of some worship and churches, but of the times when we are crying out because we have nothing else left. We feel we don't need a hero and savior and a rescue when we still have a chance. A savior rescues us when all is lost—by definition. The tough thing is that so many of us operate as if we still have a chance, when we don't—for our souls and for everything else. Enter the rope end, when we discover the truth that everything is lost without God.

Because as bad as the rope end has been, as bad as it is, it is this way for a reason. So many of us will only listen, only turn our hearts back, when we are stripped of all our hiding places and distractions, when our sins and weaknesses are made visible and clear. This is the purpose of the rope end. Not to make us feel even worse, not to run the failures highlight reel again; but because for so many, it is only then we can really say, "I need God." We reach a point where we finally and authentically say that we need Jesus for our salvation and for our living. We reach the point when we need Jesus not just recreationally, not just on Sundays, but truly, deeply and passionately—more than anything else in our lives.

It is at this point when we find ourselves searching through the closet to find the box of fading Polaroids of the God we knew or of whom we dreamed. It can be a time when we look at these and actually start to believe them. Believing that God's forgiveness is always greater than the sum total of our sins or that God is searching for the "one" and that he holds us in the palm of his hands and that he calls our names through our pain. We begin seeing a God that is making all things new and shaping us accordingly—no matter how it looks. And that he has given us the gift of a little heaven on earth through his church—no matter what people do to it.

The combination of the rope end and seeing again, or for the first time, this portrait of who God really is opens the doors to alternate endings—and really the desire for them. The desire wouldn't be there if we didn't even think it was possible. But the desire rises from this blend of purposeful desperation and possibility. And so we start thinking that forgiveness, healing, joy, strength, freedom, and hope are out there.

It becomes clear that we have come to this moment of asking for a second chance, a retry, a mulligan, a do-over with faith, with our lives, and our relationships. It is our own life and faith "Ctrl-Alt-Del" moment to reset the system. It's a God-designed moment, the one he has been guiding us to and preparing us for all of our lives. It's a moment in which everything can change. It's a moment in which the Holy Spirit moves in our hearts and we finally say, "I surrender."

This is the moment in which we give God the only thing we have left—our hearts, or what is left of our hearts— the pieces. The second chance is a surrender—the only time a surrender means victory. In every other part of life a surrender is a failure, a loss, a defeat, but to surrender to Jesus Christ is victory over all the defeats, damage, and wounds of the past. And that is when we are back. It is, in the end, a change of heart. And it may have taken years of being at the end of our rope, but it is all in God's time and way. What all seemed impossible for so long can suddenly make sense. The things we have experienced, no more and no less, have led to this moment: This heart-turn back to God.

Now, the second chance doesn't necessarily mean going back to church right now. But it is about being purposeful about finding a first or next "heaven on earth"—a body of believers that appreciate and offer second chances in Jesus's name to all. It will be about finding a church of second chances. It isn't simply praying more and reading the Bible more. Those will come in time. Right now it is about a change of heart—the rest will follow.

The authentic, real second chance is a divinely guided heart-decision that is made from the emptiness, brokenness, and desperation of the end of the rope, while embracing or grasping the truth of God's character as revealed in Scripture and in the knowledge of the promise of newer life in Jesus.

Because the amazing grace of God in Jesus Christ is this—as far away as we are or we go from God—whether it is dozens of years or thousands of miles or sins—the return is always just one step—one step back to him in our hearts.

You took my hand in the beginning of this book for comfort and encouragement and I thank you so much for trusting and listening to me. But now I need to let go, let you go. The Father is waiting to take your hand and your heart. But before you go, would you do one more thing with me? Could we say this prayer together … .

# A Second Chance Prayer

*O God, I come before you today in prayer like never before. I have realized a few things. I have realized that I am at the end of my rope and I have become a prisoner to fear, addictions, shame, desires, rage, guilt, and other soul-killers. I am telling you that I have sinned against you, and I am so sorry. I ask you to forgive me.*

*Even worse, all of this has made me distort who you really are. When I thought you had abandoned me, you were right there beside me. When I thought you had rejected me, you never stopped loving me. When I believed that I was no longer worthy of you, you didn't let me go. When I was hiding from you, you were calling out my name and looking for me. When others were judging me, you protected me. When I felt like I was broken beyond repair, you were holding the pieces ready to restore me. When I felt like an outcast from church and from others, you welcomed and remembered me. When I felt like I had hit bottom, in fact it was you holding me in your hand. When I put so many other things in front of you, your light still shined around them. I am so sorry for denying and distorting you in my mind and words and actions; I ask for your forgiveness.*

*O God, at the same time I acknowledge that only you make all things new. Thanks to Jesus, forgiveness, healing, peace, sight, renewal, freedom, and real joy can all be mine. My past, all my brokenness, all my mistakes can fall away and fade from your sight.*

*I see that "yet even now" this restart is available to me only through your son Jesus Christ, who walked this earth, bled and died on the cross for my sins, and rose again—that I might also share in resurrection. I am ready now to ask you today for a second chance, a do-over. I surrender to your love and grace this moment; I recognize that by surrendering to you, the power of the Holy Spirit is breaking through and, as promised, you will forgive me, restore my soul, and reshape my heart.*

*And so, in the name of Jesus, I humbly ask that you give me a second chance with you, with my life, and with others. I ask this knowing that nothing will ever be the same; that at this very moment you are filling my heart and soul and transforming them even as I pray. I ask this knowing that it is the beginning of the end of my old ways. I ask this knowing that all my life you have been waiting and knowing that this day, this very moment, would come right now as you had planned. I ask this in awe of your care and providence and love for me.*

*Father, I pledge and promise forevermore to belong to you above all people and things; I know this will not be easy, I know there will be more trials, wounds, and doubts; I know I will have to ask for third, fourth, fifth and many more chances. But it is different now. This second chance has changed me from the inside this time. It has changed my heart. Now, my heart belongs to you. I see now that nothing in this world can take the place of you in my life. Thank you, my Lord and my God.*

*Amen.*

# Resources

Bible Resource
www.blueletterbible.com

Prison Fellowship Ministries
www.prisonfellowship.org
877-478-0100

Young Life
www.younglife.org
877-438-9572

Intervarsity Christian Fellowship
www.intervarsity.org
608-274-9001

National Domestic Violence Hotline
www.ndvh.org
800-799-7233

Alcoholics Anonymous
www.alcoholics-anonymous.org
212-870-3400

National Institute of Mental Health
www.nimh.org
866-615-6464

Partnership for a Drug Free America
www.drugfree.org
212-922-15660

National Coalition for the Protection
of Children and Families
(Assistance with pornography addictions)
www.nationalcoalition.org
513-521-6227

Focus on the Family
(Assistance with reconciliation with spouses and family
members)
www.family.org
800-A-FAMILY (232-6459)

# NOTES

**Chapter 2**
[1] Weisel, Elie. *Night.* New York, NY: Bantam Books,1982, p. 109.

**Chapter 3**
[1] Bradshaw, John. *Healing the Shame That Binds You.* Deerfield Beach, FL: Health Communications Inc., 1988, p. 73.

**Chapter 4**
[1] Midler, Bette. "The Wind Beneath My Wings." *Beaches: Original Soundtrack Recording.* Atlantic/Wea. 1988.
[2] Eisenberg, Arlene, Heidi E. Murkoff, and Sandee E. Hathaway, B.S.N., *What To Expect The First Year.* New York, NY: Workman Publishing, 1989, 1996, p. 122.
[3] *The New Encylopedia of Christian Quotations,* compiled by Mark Water. Grand Rapids, MI: Baker Books, 2000, p. 111.
[4] Taylor, Jeannie St. John. *Am I Praying?* Grand Rapids, MI: Kregel Kidzone, 2003.
[5] *What To Expect The First Year,* op. cit., p. 367.

**Chapter 5**
[1] Sherman, Neil. *Youthful Anger Means Early Heart Disease.* Diseases and Conditions, HealthAtoZ.com, May 31, 2002.
[2] Augsbuger, David W. "Anger and Aggression," *Clinical Handbook of Pastoral Counseling, Volume I, Expanded Edition.* New York: NY: Integration Books, Paulist Press, 1985, p. 482.

**Chapter 6**
[1] Knapp, Caroline. *Drinking: A Love Story.* New York: NY: The Dial Press, 1996, p. 9.

**Chapter 8**
[1] Fact Sheet. www.selfstorage.org; Self Storage Association, April, 2006.

**Chapter 11**
[1] Wurtzel, Elizabeth. *Prozac Nation: Young and Depressed in America.* New York: NY: Riverhead, 1995, p. 3.

## Chapter 15

[1] "Miracle," Revell Bible Dictionary. Old Tappan: NJ: Fleming H. Revell Company, 1990, p.699.

## Chapter 16

[1] Williams, Margery. *The Velveteen Rabbit, Or, How Toys Become Real: The Children's Classic Edition.* Philadelphia, PA: Running Press, Courage Books, 1997, pp. 12–13.

## Chapter 18

[1] From *Star Trek II, The Wrath of Khan,* 1982.

## Chapter 19

[1] Bonhoeffer, Dietrich. *Life Together, Translated by and with an Introduction by John W. Doberstein.* New York: NY: Harper & Row Publishers, Inc., 1954, p. 30.

[2] Patton, John. *Pastoral Care in Context: An Introduction to Pastoral Care.* Louisville, KY: Westminster/John Knox Press, 1993, p.6.

[3] Ibid. p. 24.

## Chapter 22

[1] Patton, op. cit., p. 35.

## Chapter 29

[1] Bradshaw, John. *Healing the Shame That Binds You.* Deerfield Beach, FL: Health Communications Inc., 1988, p. 119.

## Chapter 34

[1] *The New Encylopedia of Christian Quotations,* compiled by Mark Water. Grand Rapids, MI: Baker Books, 2000, p. 374.

[2] *The New Encylopedia of Christian Quotations,* op. cit., p. 376.

## Chapter 35

[1] *The New Encylopedia of Christian Quotations,* op. cit., p. 536.

[2] *The New Encylopedia of Christian Quotations,* op. cit., pp. 537–538.

## Chapter 36

[1] This chapter is a narrative based on Luke 15:11–32.

# THANKSGIVING

"Beloved, I do not consider that I
have made it on my own;"
—Philippians 3:13

I thank my God, my savior Jesus Christ, and my sustainer the Holy Spirit. Without them I am nothing. I thank my helpmate, my love, my coach, my first editor, my best friend and wife, Jennifer: Her support, efforts, and patience literally make this ministry and book possible. And my joys, Brian and Madelyn: You are God's greatest gifts to me—without you it wouldn't mean anything.

I give thanks for all my family and friends who have prayed for this book and for me over the last year. I could feel your prayers encouraging me.

I give thanks to following congregations for their prayers, love, and support: First Reformed Church of Grandville, Michigan; Lebanon Reformed Church of Lebanon, New Jersey; Reformed Church of North Brunswick, New Jersey; Hillsborough Reformed Church at Millstone, New Jersey; Middlebush Reformed Church of Somerset, New Jersey; and St. Anne's Parish of Fair Lawn, New Jersey.

I thank my literary agent Tim Beals, of Credo Communications, for his faith and encouragement. I thank Dirk Wierenga, Ginny McFadden, and Jennifer Phipps of FaithWalk Publishing.

"I thank my God every time I remember you."
—Philippians 1:3

# ABOUT THE AUTHOR

Christopher B. Wolf is the beneficiary of many second chances and do-overs in his faith and life. Christopher believes his calling is to reach out to the broken and hurting as an instrument of hope and encouragement. He has led churches in New Jersey and Michigan and is known for his compassionate, dynamic leadership as well as for communicating biblical truths with insight and passion. He grew up as a Roman Catholic and went on to become an ordained pastor in the Reformed Church in America. Prior to entering ministry, Christopher worked in journalism, state government, and public relations. He lives in Grandville, Michigan, with his wife Jennifer and his children Brian and Madelyn. Please visit with Christopher at his web site—www.christopherbwolf.com—to share your journey or second chance story.